PLAZA

Lincoln's Land

for Haydon and Emmett …
because they asked

Lincoln's Land: The History of Abraham Lincoln's Coles County Farm
by Kurt W. Peterson

Design and layout by David Westerfield

Copyright © 2008 by Friends of the Abraham Lincoln Historical Farm LLC
All rights reserved.
Printed in the United States of America
ISBN 978-1-60725-571-0

Friends of the Abraham Lincoln Historical Farm LLC
1620 Colonial Parkway
Inverness, Illinois 60067

Lincoln's Land

The History of Abraham Lincoln's Coles County Farm

by Kurt W. Peterson

Friends of the
Abraham Lincoln Historical Farm LLC

CONTENTS

FOREWORD

Abraham Lincoln spent the first twenty-two years of his life on farms that were located very near the frontier line in Kentucky, Indiana and Illinois. His father farmed but depended upon his carpentry skills to augment a somewhat tenuous living. Actually, Thomas Lincoln appears to have been a rather average head of household in the regions where he resided.

Until he was twenty-one, young Abraham was sometimes hired out to neighbors for wages which his father kept. That was the usual practice in that era. Abraham seems to have resented this garnishment of his pay when he remarked that he was once a slave but was now so free that they allowed him to practice law! However, Abraham probably got along with his father as well as other youngsters of his time.

Long after Abraham Lincoln left agricultural pursuits, the language of rural farmsteads continued to color his speech and writings. Since a majority of the United States population had either been born on farms or were still farming in Lincoln's lifetime, he was always understood and appreciated as one of their own. Many of his famous stories also stemmed from his time in the country, splitting rails or planting and harvesting. Although as a politician, Lincoln downplayed his hunting experience, close friends of his youth declared that he did hunt with them and even drank a bit of whiskey upon occasion. Indeed, one might say that he was "one of the boys," and a very popular one too.

Professor Kurt W. Peterson of North Park University in Chicago has related Abraham Lincoln's farm background in *Lincoln's Land: The History of Abraham Lincoln's Coles County Farm*. This publication, sponsored by Friends of the Abraham Lincoln Historical Farm LLC, is intended to accompany deeds to small sections of land from the Abraham Lincoln Forty which Lawyer Lincoln purchased in 1841 so his lenient father could prevent his stepson from selling it and thus depriving Abraham's stepmother of a living if Thomas died before she did. Abraham was extremely fond of Sarah (Bush) Johnston Lincoln who had assisted him in every way possible while he was growing up. She wanted him to be educated and prosperous.

Any profits derived from the sale of this little volume will be utilized for philanthropic projects in areas like education, literacy, citizenship and Illinois tourism—projects which Lincoln himself would have supported. It is a worthy cause which needs support from the public.

Wayne C. Temple, Ph.D., Chief Deputy Director of the Illinois State Archives and author of *Abraham Lincoln: From Skeptic to Prophet* and *By Square and Compass: The Saga of the Lincoln Home*

First known photograph of Abraham Lincoln. Taken by Nicholas H. Shepherd, one of the earliest photographers in Springfield, in 1846 or 1847 after Lincoln was elected to the House of Representatives. Lincoln was thirty-seven or thirty-eight at the time of this sitting. Photograph first published in *McClure's* magazine in December 1895 after Robert T. Lincoln had revealed its existence to writer Ida Tarbell when she interviewed him in Chicago early in 1895. Robert said that this photograph hung on the wall of his home from the time he could first remember. Mary Lincoln Isham, Robert's daughter, presented the original daguerreotype of Lincoln to the Library of Congress in October 1937. Courtesy of the Abraham Lincoln Presidential Library & Museum.

Lincoln's Farmland: Yesterday and Today

In the fall of 1841 Abraham Lincoln was thirty-two years old, and he was just hitting his professional groove. He was emerging as a prominent attorney in Springfield, Illinois; he had argued his first case before the Illinois Supreme Court the previous June; and in August, voters from his district reelected him to his fourth term in the Illinois legislature where he served as the Whig Party's floor leader. As his professional security grew, his mind was on his family. On October 25, 1841, Lincoln purchased a forty-acre plot of land from his parents. It was a parcel from their 120-acre "Goosenest Prairie" farm located in Coles County, Illinois, about one hundred miles east of Springfield. Legend has it that the area got its name from an early settler who compared the fertile soil to the richness of a goose egg, exclaiming, "This is the very goose-nest."

Lincoln never sold this forty-acre plot, and it was not listed on his posthumous probate inventory in 1865; so the title remained formally in his name until 1888. At that time John J. Hall, the son of Lincoln's stepsister Matilda Johnston Hall Moore, secured title to it, stating that he had held "actual, open, continued, uninterrupted, unquestioned, undisturbed, and peaceable possession" of it since 1851. The land remained in the Lincoln family until 1914 when the heirs of John J. Hall sold it to some Coles County neighbors.

That forty-acre parcel (hereafter referred to as "Lincoln's Farmland") was originally purchased from the United States government by John D. Johnston on August 4, 1837. Coles County had only recently been settled, and the previous January, Lincoln's father had purchased eighty adjacent acres to the north. He did not build a cabin on that land but instead continued to reside on his "Muddy Point" farm a few miles away. In August of 1837 when John D. Johnston bought "Lincoln's Farmland," Thomas and Sarah Bush Lincoln, having sold their "Muddy Point" farm the previous May, moved into the property's one-room cabin which had probably been built by squatters in 1835. The Lincolns lived there in crowded conditions with Sarah's son, John D. Johnston; his wife, Mary; and their two boys.

Abraham Lincoln never lived with his parents in Coles County. In 1830, they moved from Indiana to Macon County, Illinois, where they lived for one year before somewhat unintentionally settling in Coles County. (They intended to go back to Indiana and stopped in Coles Couny en route; while they were there, John Sawyer, an early settler there, convinced Thomas to stay.) Abraham did not make that trip with them. Because he was over twenty-one and therefore no longer financially obligated to his father, he had already moved away from the family. He settled first in New Salem, and then moved to Springfield a few years later after the state capitol was moved there from Vandalia in 1837.

In March of 1840, Thomas Lincoln exchanged the eighty acres of land he owned to the north of "Lincoln's Farmland" for eighty acres adjacent to its western boundary. That land was owned by Reuben Moore, Sarah Bush Lincoln's son-in-law. That fall, John D. Johnston and Thomas Lincoln decided to enlarge their living space. As John J. Hall told Eleanor Gridley, secretary of the Abraham Lincoln Log Cabin Association who

Thomas and Sarah Bush Johnston Lincoln's "Goosenest Prairie" log cabin. Courtesy of the Abraham Lincoln Presidential Library & Museum.

meticulously interviewed Lincoln's Coles County family members in 1891, Lincoln encouraged his father and stepbrother to move the old cabin from Johnston's forty acres to higher ground on the farm, and he helped them build an additional "west room" so his stepmother would be more comfortable. This would have been familiar work for Lincoln, having spent the first twenty years of his life as a farmer and assistant to his carpenter, joiner, and cabinetmaker father.

In 1891, John J. Hall sold the cabin to James W. Craig of Mattoon, who in turn sold it to the Abraham Lincoln Log Cabin Association. The association dissembled it and moved it to Chicago where it was reassembled and featured in the year-long Columbian Exposition, the 1893 Chicago World's Fair. While there were many plans for preserving and exhibiting the cabin, it remained in storage so long that promoters forgot about it and it was eventually lost to history. Some say that it was forgotten and unknowingly used as firewood. Today a replica cabin stands on the original site as confirmed by Illinois archeologists. It is part of the Lincoln Log Cabin State Historic Site in Lerna, Illinois, an eighty-six-acre living historical farm which contains Thomas Lincoln's original eighty-acre "Goosenest Prairie" farm, as well as other historic Lincoln-related buildings from the region.

Thomas Lincoln added to his landholdings on December 31, 1840, when he purchased Johnston's forty acres, or "Lincoln's Farmland," for fifty dollars. In acquiring this land, Thomas Lincoln over-stretched himself financially, and he appealed to his son for help. Abraham, in an act of filial duty and generosity, paid his father two hundred dollars for the newly acquired forty acres—four times what his father had paid for it just months earlier. Both Thomas and Sarah Bush Lincoln signed the original deed, which is now housed in the Special Collections department of the Chicago Public Library, with Sarah leaving her mark, an "X," as she never learned to read or write. This was no financially savvy real estate deal on Lincoln's part;

This historical replica of the Thomas Lincoln log cabin was built in 1935. Archaeologists, architects, and builders, working together as part of a Civilian Conservation Corps project, reconstructed the cabin in its original location, where it now stands as part of the Lincoln Log Cabin Historic Site in Lerna, Illinois. Photograph by author, 2008.

rather, it was an act of generosity toward his parents who were struggling to make a go of it on the Illinois prairie. In the agreement, Abraham reserved for his parents "the occupation, use, and entire control of said tract of land, and the appurtenances thereunto belonging" for the rest of their lives. Thus Lincoln relieved his parents' burden by buying a portion of their farm and then giving use of it right back to them. Although Lincoln never lived on his parents' Goosenest Prairie farm, he visited a few times and, because his beloved stepmother lived there for years after his father's death, he considered it in many ways to be home. Sarah lived on the land until her death in 1869.

In 2007, Daniel Arnold, president of Friends of the Abraham Lincoln Historical Farm LLC, purchased four acres of the original "Lincoln's Farmland"—a swath of land adjacent to the eastern border of today's Lincoln Log Cabin State Historic Site. The land's previous owner had lost most of the forty-acre plot through risky business ventures in the 1970s. After significant research, Arnold decided to purchase Lincoln's land to preserve it for posterity and to promote the values that made Lincoln great and which remain at the core of the United States. Arnold wanted to give the land back to the American public in remembrance of Illinois's beloved president. "I purchased the farm in order to use it to help charities, to promote the character virtues of Abraham Lincoln to future generations, and to help promote tourism in the state of Illinois," Arnold explains. The land is now owned and operated by Friends of the Abraham Lincoln Historical Farm LLC. To accomplish Arnold's vision, that organization is recording common undivided interests in the land and publishing this book, making them available to the public. It is the organization's belief that this historic asset should not be owned or kept in private hands, but rather, in tribute to Lincoln, should belong to the public and serve the common good.*

* *To purchase a piece of the farm, visit www.lincolnfamilyfarm.com or call 1-888-OWN-FARM*

Photo taken by Christopher S. German in Springfield, Illinois, on January 13, 1861, just days prior to Lincoln's visit to Coles County. Taken at the request of sculptor Thomas Jones, who came to Springfield to make a bust of Lincoln. Courtesy of the Abraham Lincoln Presidential Library & Museum.

CHAPTER ONE

Lincoln's Final Visit to His Family's "Goosenest Prairie" Farm

O n Wednesday morning, January 30, 1861, Abraham Lincoln boarded a Great Western Railroad car in Springfield, Illinois, for the arduous hundred-mile trip to Coles County where he would visit his beloved stepmother for the last time. He came also to pay his respects at the grave of his father, who had died ten years earlier, to spend time with his large extended family, and to see one last time the rough-hewn cabin on the Goosenest Prairie where his family had lived since the 1830s. Lincoln would switch trains in Mattoon and arrive on a frieght train in Charleston, Illinois, the county seat, after six o'clock that evening.

The weight of the world was on Lincoln's shoulders. Since winning the presidential election two months earlier, he had received scores of death threats from disgruntled southerners. Six states (South Carolina, Mississippi, Florida, Alabama, Georgia, and Louisiana) had already seceded from the Union. In a week's time, those states, along with Texas, which would secede while Lincoln was visiting Coles County, would form the Confederate States of America. Three weeks earlier, the first shots of what

Cannons fire on Fort Sumter. Illustration included in the April 27, 1861, edition of *Harper's Weekly* which featured a biography and picture of President Abraham Lincoln, and a description of Mr. Lincoln's declaration of war on the south.

would become a full-fledged civil war had been fired in Charleston Harbor by a group of Citadel cadets. They had battered the sloop *Star of the West,* keeping it from resupplying Major Robert Anderson's troops stationed off the South Carolina coast at Fort Sumter. Lincoln had spent the previous weeks receiving an endless stream of office seekers and politicians at his Springfield home, and he had just completed the first draft of his first inaugural address. In the midst of this troubling chaos, he traveled to Coles County to see his family.

Lincoln arrived at the Charleston Depot dressed unassumingly and without bodyguards. The train let him off a hundred feet from the platform, forcing the president-elect to trudge through deep mud from the day's winter rains before he climbed up onto the wooden planks. One observer remarked simply, "There were no formalities." Although Lincoln would greet many well-wishers and office-seekers, he was coming to town for personal reasons. After shaking hands with a number of townspeople who had gathered to greet him, he left for state senator Thomas A. Marshall's home where he would dine, greet scores of political callers, and spend the night. Early the next morning, Lincoln had breakfast at the home of Dennis Hanks, his mother's cousin and dear childhood friend. He left directly from there in a horse-drawn buggy with Augustus H. Chapman, Hanks's son-in-law, for the Lincoln farm.

The two men traveled the seven or so miles to the Farmington home of Reuben and Matilda Moore, Sarah Bush Johnston Lincoln's daughter. Lincoln's stepmother was staying with the Moores because the chimney in her Goosenest Prairie cabin, which some historians think Lincoln helped his father build in the 1830s, had collapsed the day before. A few years later, Chapman would recollect Lincoln's words while they rode toward the Moore home: "Mr. Lincoln spoke to me…of his stepmother in the most affectionate manner. Said she had been his best friend in this world

Sarah Bush Johnston Lincoln (1788-1869), Lincoln's stepmother. Photograph taken around 1864 in Charleston, Illinois when Sarah was seventy-six years old. It was owned by Harriet (Hanks) Chapman, Lincoln's step-niece. Although many copies of the image exist, the whereabouts of the original are unknown. Courtesy of the Abraham Lincoln Presidential Library & Museum.

and that no man could love a mother more than he loved her." Lincoln's own mother had died when he was just nine years old. His father, Thomas Lincoln, married Sarah Bush Johnston the following year, and she brought order, love, laughter, and encouragement into a cold Lincoln household.

Lincoln's stepmother took an immediate liking to young Abe, remarking later in life that "Abe was the best boy I ever saw or ever hope to see." Their mutual admiration was so special, she said once, "I never gave him a cross word in all my life." Another time she lovingly noted, "His mind and

Thomas Lincoln. Photograph was originally owned by Lieutenant O. V. Flora, who served in the Tenth Ohio Battery from Springfield, Ohio. While in Charleston, Illinois, he bought the photograph from someone close to the Lincoln family who claimed it to be an authentic image of Thomas Lincoln. Courtesy of the Abraham Lincoln Museum of Lincoln Memorial University, Harrogate, Tennessee.

mine—what little I had—seemed to move together—move in the same channel." Lincoln would remark on another occasion to William Herndon, his Springfield law partner, "All that I am, or hope to be, I owe to my angel [step]mother." Although she could not read or write, Sarah encouraged young Abe in his studies, even cajoling Thomas to be more patient with his son's studious inclinations. As memory of his mother, Nancy Hanks Lincoln, faded, Lincoln came to adore his stepmother, giving her credit for the person he came to be.

When Lincoln finally reached her that morning in 1861, he took his stepmother in his arms and she embraced her beloved "Abe." John J. Hall, Sarah's grandson, recollected, "She cried over him. She told him that day it would be the last time she would see him, and he tried to pacify her. 'Why mother?' he asked, and she said, 'Abe, you are such a good man that they will kill you.' He only laughed." After that brief greeting, Lincoln and Chapman took the horse and buggy to visit the grave of Thomas Lincoln at Shilo Cemetery. But first, the historical record seems to indicate, they stopped by the Lincoln farmstead, the "Goosenest Prairie." Thomas Lincoln had lived on this land for twenty years before his death in 1851, and Sarah, along with other family members, continued to live there.

On that cold January day, Lincoln stepped onto his family's Goosenest Prairie farm for the last time. As he looked through the winter forest, across the prairie toward the Embarrass River, and breathed in the brisk country air, perhaps Lincoln pondered the many turns his life had taken up to that point. After spending the first twenty-two years of his life farming in Kentucky and Indiana, he had since worked as a store clerk, postmaster, surveyor, captain in the Illinois militia during the Black Hawk War (1832), state representative, Illinois congressman, and attorney. He now had a wife and family of his own, had been elected president of the United States, and would soon take the oath of office in the midst of a profound national crisis. Before he headed to the cemetery to visit his father's grave, he might have looked out over the land, his land, and reflected on his strained but respectful relationship with his father. Maybe he dreamed of a life of quiet, pastoral simplicity invitingly whispering to him from the sparse, silent landscape. As he walked "Lincoln's Farmland," perhaps he thought of his love for his parents, which had motivated him to buy the land for them. Much must have been on his mind, but he did not linger long. He had to get back to the Moore home for a dinner with family and neighborhood friends.

By the time Lincoln and Chapman returned to the Moore home, a large crowd of friends and neighbors had gathered to greet him. R. H. Osbourne, the local schoolteacher, dismissed class and brought his students over to the Moore home so they could shake hands with the president-elect.

Sarah Bush Lincoln's granddaughter, Sarah Louisa Hall Fox, would recall later that there were present at the dinner party "people from every walk of life there abouts, ministers and railsplitters come right from the wood." Lincoln stood at the door, greeting each person with a handshake, and then went into the living room to eat dinner on tables fashioned from planks and sawhorses. Throughout the evening Lincoln's face was filled with smiles as he recounted stories from his youth. After dinner, he took a long walk with his now-aged stepmother. Her daughter and granddaughter accompanied them. As the walk ended Sarah embraced Lincoln and said, "My dear boy, I always thought there was something great in you. With this war coming on, I am afraid you are going to have a hard time." Another person present at the dinner party recounted her words as even more ominous: "Abe, I'll never see you again. They will kill you." Lincoln responded, "Don't worry. Everything will come out all right."

Years later, a few months after Lincoln was assassinated, his stepmother remarked to Lincoln's law partner, William Henry Herndon:

> I did not want to see Abe run for President, did not want him elected, was afraid, somehow or other, felt it in my heart that something would happen to him, and when he came down to see me after he was elected President, I still felt that something told me that something would befall Abe and that I should see him no more. Abe and his father are in Heaven, I have no doubt, and I want to go to them, go where they are. God bless Abraham.

The historical record is unclear, but it appears that Sarah accepted an invitation from Augustus Chapman and accompanied him and Lincoln back to Charleston so she could remain with Abraham until his train departed the following morning. When they arrived in Charleston, a large crowd had gathered in the town hall to see the president-elect—neighbors and friends who wanted to wish him well and say good-bye. Although some requested that he make a political statement on the state of the country, Lincoln declined and instead verbally cavorted with the audience for hours. In an unexpected serendipity, he spent the whole evening with friends remembering his youth and young adulthood, listening to stories and recollections. Lincoln's law partner later wrote:

> In the audience were many persons who had known him first as the stalwart young ox-driver when his father's family drove into Illinois from southern Indiana. One man had brought with him a horse which the president-elect, in the earlier days of his law practice, had recovered for him in a replevin suit; another one was able to recite from personal recollection the thrilling details of the famous wrestling match between Lincoln the flatboatman in 1830 and Daniel Needham; and all had some reminiscence of his early manhood to relate.

One city resident present at that meeting noted that although Lincoln was generally "cheerful," his face occasionally lit up "by the recital of some of his inimitable stories," he exhibited the "grave face for which he was noted." Lincoln probably suspected what lay ahead. After spending two weeks in Springfield, he proceeded toward Washington D.C., making many stops along the way. One week after Lincoln formally took office, General P.G.T. Beauregard opened fire on Fort Sumter, launching the American Civil War.

After sharing that evening with friends, Lincoln arose early the next morning to say good-bye and head to the train station. As Chapman remembered, when Lincoln said good-bye to his stepmother, she once again spoke presciently of his impending death. Their parting "was very affectionate." She embraced him when they parted and said she would never be permitted to see him again, that she felt his enemies would assassinate

him. He replied…"no no Mama (he always called her Mama) they will not do that. Trust in the Lord and all will be well. We will see each other again." Chapman would later reflect on Lincoln's visit to Coles County in 1861 saying, "Mr. Lincoln appeared to enjoy his visit here remarkable well. His reception by his old acquaintances appeared to be very gratifying to him. They all appeared glad to see him, and all appeared so anxious that his administration might be a success

Lincoln bids farewell to his mother in 1861, just weeks before he leaves to take the oath of office as the sixteenth president of the United States. Illustration by Lloyd Ostendorf.

and that he might have a pleasant and honorable career as president."

Having been wished well by his friends and family, Lincoln headed to the nation's capitol where, on March 4, 1861, he delivered his first inaugural address. Included in that speech are some of the most memorable words in American rhetoric. After defending the Constitution and clearly communicating his unswerving commitment to the Union, he assured the nation that he was not seeking to manipulate the people through abuses of executive power, affirming that great founding principle that American government emerges from the citizens themselves. He asked, "Why should there not be a patient confidence in the ultimate justice of the people? Is there any better or equal hope in the world?" He then turned to his southern brothers and sisters who had seceded and were preparing for war. With a tinge of the melancholy that characterized his public life, Lincoln mused,

I am loath to close. We are not enemies, but friends. We must not be enemies. Though passion may have strained it must not break our bonds of affection. The mystic chords of memory, stretching from every battlefield and patriot grave to every living heart and hearthstone all over this broad land, will yet swell the chorus of the Union, when again touched, as surely they will be, by the better angels of our nature.

Lincoln pleaded with the American people to show one another humaneness, compassion, good will, and tolerance so that they might honor the sacrifices of previous patriots by preserving national unity. It was such traits that Lincoln learned from his family and tried to exhibit throughout his life.

Historian Charles H. Coleman, in his book *Abraham Lincoln and Coles County, Illinois,* has remarked, "This visit ... probably was the most pleasant and satisfying incident in Lincoln's life from the time of his election to his death in April, 1865. ... The visit revived and refreshed the tired and worried Lincoln, exhausted by the importunities of office-seekers and deeply troubled by the grave responsibilities he was about to assume." His visit was not only refreshing and personally satisfying, it revealed his core personality and strong character. When Lincoln made this visit to family a high priority, immediately before assuming the presidency, he revealed the love for his family that he had exhibited all his life. Although his relationship with his father was often strained, largely because Lincoln wanted to leave a life of rural poverty behind him, he remained loyal to his parents and extended family. He regularly visited them, provided financial assistance, and housed family members in his Springfield home. No matter how high he climbed, Lincoln always remembered where he came from.

Humility and filial piety are two of Lincoln's virtues often noted by historians. Eventually, a legendary log-splitter of uncommon character, born in a log cabin in northern Kentucky, would be mythically remembered for his honesty, hard work, persistence, humanity, oratory skill, dogged pursuit of self-education, commitment to justice, and tireless defense of democracy. While it is often difficult to find the "real" Lincoln amidst all the lofty panegyrics and ruthless denunciations penned by fans and detractors alike, most agree that Lincoln was a person of uncommon integrity. Historians routinely rank him first among American presidents, and societies dedicated to preserving his legacy abound.

While the land Abraham Lincoln bought from his father is the subject of this work, this book is about much more than the land itself. In order to understand Lincoln's connection to this Coles County farmland, one must first understand his upbringing and boyhood experience as a frontier farmer. In these pages we will consider his connection to Coles County, his family, and the virtues he modeled for the American public.

Photograph taken in February 1864 by Anthony Berger, later used as the basis for Lincoln's image on the five-dollar bill. Courtesy of the Abraham Lincoln Presidential Library & Museum.

CHAPTER TWO

Lincoln's Life on the Land: From Kentucky to Indiana

When Abraham Lincoln reached twenty-two years of age, he left the family farm, never to return. Up until that point any money he had made farming, splitting rails, working in a mill, or sailing flat boats to distant markets legally belonged to his father. When he reached the age of maturity, it is clear, Lincoln wanted a different life. An avid reader, debater, and storyteller, he desired an escape from the monotonous demands of farm labor. As historian Wayne C. Temple has observed, Lincoln indeed "desired to put his agricultural experiences behind him as quickly as possible once he had fled from farming," and he "hated the hard labor and low remuneration" characteristic of frontier life. However, while Lincoln wanted to move beyond the life of an unsophisticated dirt farmer, Temple reminds us that "he was what he was no matter how hard he might desire to forget his past heritage."

Some historians overemphasize Lincoln's disdain for rural life, claiming he had deep contempt for his uneducated, laboring father, and only scorn for his frontier past. While it is true that as a youth Lincoln preferred to read a book than to swing an axe, such claims do not recognize that Lincoln continued to think like a man of the soil throughout his career. He often used the language of the farming life to communicate the virtues he had learned during his frontier childhood. Lincoln's practical concern for his parents, revealed in his purchase of "Lincoln's Farmland," and his frequent references to the importance of land ownership and the accompanying hard work needed to develop it, indicate that he remained a farmer in spirit his entire life. Though he never farmed them, during his adult life Lincoln owned plots of farmland in Iowa and Illinois, and he ended his life reflecting on the pastoral qualities of farming life.

Toward the end of the Civil War, Lincoln met in his White House office with Captain Russell Conwell regarding the fate of one of his young soldiers who had been sentenced to death for military discipline. Conwell had responded to stirring speeches by Henry Ward Beecher and Abraham Lincoln by enlisting in the Union army in 1862. He would eventually become one of the nation's most prominent Protestant ministers and deliver his self-help lecture, "Acres of Diamonds," more than 6,000 times during the late nineteenth century. In that lecture he recounted his meeting with the president. Conwell timidly entered Lincoln's office and sat on the edge of a chair while the president finished some paperwork. Conwell described their encounter:

> Finally, when he put the string around his papers, he pushed them over to one side and looked over at me, and a smile came over his worn face. He said: "I am a very busy man and have only a few minutes to spare. Now tell me in the fewest words what it is you want." I began to tell him, and mentioned the case, and he said: "I have heard all about it and you do not need to say any more. Mr. Stanton was talking to me only a few days ago about that. You can go to the hotel and rest assured that the President never did sign an order to shoot a boy under twenty years of

age, and never will. You can say that to his mother anyhow."

Then Lincoln asked,

> "How is it going in the field?" I said, "We sometimes get discouraged." And he said: "It is all right. We are going to win out now. We are getting very near the light. No man ought to wish to be President of the United States, and I will be glad when I get through; then Tad and I are going out to Springfield, Illinois. I have bought a farm out there and I don't care if I again earn only twenty-five cents a day. Tad has a mule team, and we are going to plant onions."

The two men then began to talk about life on the farm. Lincoln asked Conwell, "Were you brought up on a farm?" When Conwell said that he had grown up on a farm in the Berkshires in Massachusetts, Lincoln "then threw his leg over the corner of the big chair and said, 'I have heard many a time, ever since I was young, that up there in those hills you have to sharpen the noses of the sheep in order to get down to the grass between the rocks.'" Conwell remembered their interaction fondly, saying, "He was so familiar, so everyday, so farmer-like, that I felt right at home with him at once." As a melancholy Lincoln faced the troubles of leading the nation through its most profound moral and military crisis, he returned to the pastoral themes of his youth where he found solace and peace. Even as the nation's supreme statesman, he remained "farmer-like," able to relate clearly to a young soldier. Lincoln was a lawyer, small business owner, politician, and president, but he remained a man of the land.

Abraham Lincoln grew up poor on the hardscrabble American frontier. In 1860 when Lincoln was running for president, John Locke Scripps of the *Chicago Tribune* asked him for information he might use to write his campaign biography. Lincoln told him, "Why Scripps, ... it is a great piece of folly to attempt to make anything out of my early life. It can all be condensed into a single sentence, and that sentence you will find in Gray's Elegy: 'the short and simple annals of the poor.' That's my life, and that's all you or any one else can make of it." Lincoln knew little about his ancestry, never doing much research into his family background. Perhaps that was because, as Lincoln biographer David Herbert Donald argues, he did not care much about his family tree, being more interested in making himself into a new person. Or, perhaps it was because Abraham Lincoln assumed no one else would care about his humble beginnings.

Nancy Hanks Lincoln (1784-1818), Abraham Lincoln's mother who died of the "milk sickness" when the family lived in Indiana. Copyright 1963 by Lloyd Ostendorf.

Abraham Lincoln was born in a log cabin with a dirt floor on the banks of Nolin Creek near Hodgenville, Kentucky, on February 12, 1809, to Thomas and Nancy Hanks Lincoln, who had wed three years earlier. He joined his two-year-old sister, Sarah, who later would die in childbirth at the age of twenty in Indiana. His mother's family, a group of largely illiterate farmers of modest means, had moved from Virginia to Kentucky around 1780. His father's family had also moved from Virginia to Kentucky around the same time. Lincoln's paternal grandfather, Abraham Lincoln, was a man of more significant means, at one point owning more than 5,000 acres of land in one of the richest sections of Kentucky. The family's original North American Lincoln ancestor, Samuel Lincoln, immigrated from the County of Norfolk in England to Hingham, Massachusetts, in 1637 as part of the great migration that began when the Puritans landed in Massachusetts Bay seven years earlier. Samuel became a prosperous trader and businessman, and some of his descendants joined the economic elite. As historian David Herbert Donald put it, "Abraham Lincoln, instead of being the unique blossom on an otherwise barren family tree, belonged to the seventh American generation of a family with competent means, a reputation for integrity, and a modest record of public service."

In 1786, the young Thomas Lincoln learned firsthand the tenuousness of frontier life when his father was killed by Indians who were violently opposed to white settlement on the extending frontier. Carl Sandburg recounts the story:

> One day [Abraham] was working in a field with his three sons, and they saw him in a spasm of pain fall to the ground, just after the boys had heard a rifle shot and the whine of a bullet. The boys yelled to each other, "Indians!" Mordecai ran to a cabin nearby, Josiah started across fields and woods to a fort to bring help. Six-year-old Tom stooped over his father's bleeding body and wondered what he could do. He looked up to see an Indian standing over him, a shining bangle hanging down over the Indian's shoulder close to the heart. Then Tom saw the Indian's hands clutch upward, saw him double with a groan and crumple to the ground. Mordecai with a rifle at a peephole in the cabin had aimed his shot at the shining bangle. Little Tom was so near he heard the bullet plug its hole into the red man.

As he grew up, Thomas Lincoln lived in several different places in Kentucky among relatives, and learned skills as a farmer, carpenter, cabinetmaker, and millworker along the way. Because of his father's early death, Thomas had no chance to become the heir of a wealthy planter. Instead

Abraham Lincoln's birthplace. This cabin, housed in the Memorial Building at the Abraham Lincoln Birthplace National Historic Site (Hodgenville, Kentucky) is believed to be the birthplace of Abraham Lincoln, the so-called "Sinking Springs Farm" cabin. Lincoln lived in this cabin from 1809-1811.

he had to work hard to save enough money to buy his first farm—a 238-acre tract on Mill Creek in Hardin County, Kentucky, near Elizabethtown. In 1809, Thomas moved his wife, Nancy, and two-year-old Sarah to a 300-acre farm on the banks of Nolin Creek. Abraham was born there that February. Lincoln biographer and United States senator (Indiana) Albert J. Beveridge described the cabin Thomas Lincoln built on this "Sinking Spring Farm":

> The earth was the floor of that shelter. The roof of rough slabs was held in place by poles and stones. In the log walls a small

square opening, possibly covered with greased paper, let in a scant, dim light. Two long, broad slabs, fastened together and attached by hinges of wood or of hide to the side of a cut in the walls high enough for man to pass through, served as a door.

At one end of this cabin was a rude fireplace of stone with a chimney of sticks and clay. In a corner opposite was a pallet or bed, the frame made by a crotched stick driven into the ground upon which the ends of a long and short pole rested, the other ends thrust between the logs of the cabin. Across this frame were placed rough slats, and upon these bedding of some sort was spread. The whole structure was of wood, no iron being available.

Thomas quickly learned that although the setting of the Sinking Springs farm was beautiful, the land was not suitable for farming and thus would not support his family. In the spring of 1811 the family moved to a smaller but more fertile farm ten miles to the northeast on Knob Creek. Here the family lived for five years in a one-room cabin. Abraham's earliest memories came from this period. He would recall working in the "big field" planting and harvesting corn and pumpkins, as well as two brief periods when he attended an "ABC School" where he learned the alphabet. The Lincoln family left Kentucky for Indiana in 1816 when Abraham was just seven years old.

Thomas Lincoln decided to leave Kentucky for two key reasons: he had encountered legal difficulty securing proper title to his land, resulting in constant court battles; and he was opposed to the institution of slavery which was legal and extensive throughout the state. He opposed slavery on both religious and economic grounds. He and Nancy joined a Separate Baptist Church that morally opposed slavery, and as a small farmer he found himself in economic competition with slave-owning planters. For Thomas Lincoln, as became true for his son, slavery was an impediment to

Abraham Lincoln's boyhood home in Kentucky. This historically preserved "Knob Creek" cabin is located approximately ten miles from the Abraham Lincoln Birthplace National Historic Site in Hodgenville, Kentucky. Lincoln and his family lived in this home from 1811 until 1816 when the family moved to Indiana.

fair, open competition that rewarded hard work, thrift, and industry, rather than inherited wealth or privilege. Indiana, which was determined to be free territory in the Northwest Ordinance of 1787, became a free state in 1816 (the year of the Lincoln migration). By moving there, Thomas Lincoln could distance himself from the institution of slavery, thus allowing him to build a future for himself and his family on his own merits.

Just as important in his decision to move to Indiana was Thomas Lincoln's difficulty in acquiring secure title to his land. Kentucky was settled early without the structure of a formal land survey which would have made holdings clear. Because the land was settled in chaotic fashion, the courts were always clogged with legal battles among neighbors and investors. Thomas Lincoln himself was unable to establish clear title on any of his three Kentucky farms. Thus Indiana became the land of opportunity for him and his family.

There, the family settled in the wilderness on Pigeon Creek, in Perry (later Spencer) County, in southern Indiana. Thomas preceded his family, chose the land, and built a "half-faced camp" where they would live while he and Abe built the family cabin. In his 1860 campaign autobiography, Lincoln, writing in the third person, recounted those back-breaking Indiana years.

> [Thomas Lincoln and his family] settled in an unbroken forest, and the clearing away of surplus wood was the great task ahead. Abraham, though very young, was large of his age, and had an ax put into his hands at once; and from that till within his twenty-third year he was almost constantly handling that most useful instrument—less, of course, in plowing and harvesting seasons. At this place Abraham took an early start as a hunter, which was never much improved afterward. A few days before the completion of his eighth year, in the absence of his father, a flock of wild turkeys approached the new log cabin, and Abraham with a rifle-gun, standing inside, shot through a crack and killed one of them. He has never since pulled a trigger on any larger game.

After a lonely year, the Lincoln family was joined in Indiana by Elizabeth (Hanks) and Thomas Sparrow (Nancy Hanks Lincoln's aunt and uncle) and Dennis Hanks (Elizabeth Sparrow's nephew).

The Lincoln and Sparrow families had been in Indiana only a short time before tragedy struck. Having hooked his mare to Gordon's gristmill, where he had taken the family's corn to be ground into meal, young Abe lashed the horse in order to quicken its pace. The angry horse kicked him in the forehead, and Abe fell to the ground, bleeding and unconscious. Bystanders came to his aid, but judging him to be dead, ran off to get his father. When

Abraham Lincoln's cousins, Dennis and John Hanks, standing in front of the Lincoln home in Macon County, Illinois, which Abraham helped build in 1830. The logs for the cabin were cut by John Hanks. Years later, Dennis Hanks would recall, "Abe helped put up a cabin fur Tom [his father] on the Sangamon, clear fifteen acres fur carn an' split rails to fence it in....We lived jest like the Indians, 'cept we talked religion and politics." Picture from the Ostendorf Collection.

Dennis Hanks (1799-1892), cousin to John Hanks and Nancy Hanks Lincoln, and a close childhood friend to Abraham Lincoln. He lived with the Lincoln family in Indiana from 1818 to 1821 when he married Sarah Elizabeth Johnston, daughter of Sarah Bush Johnston Lincoln. Picture from the Ostendorf collection.

John Hanks (1802-1899), cousin of Nancy Hanks Lincoln, who lived with the Lincoln family in Indiana for four years. He preceded Thomas Lincoln to Macon County, Illinois, encouraging Thomas to move his family there in 1830. It was John Hanks who joined Lincoln and John D. Johnston on the flatboat trip sponsored by Denton Offutt to New Orleans in 1831. Picture from the Ostendorf collection.

Thomas arrived he found his son unconscious but alive. Abraham could not speak for several hours, but he recovered and suffered no permanent damage. One theory maintains that this blow to the head accounts for the peculiar structural irregularities of Lincoln's face. A multimedia presentation at the Abraham Lincoln Presidential Museum in Springfield, Illinois, notes the unusual fact that Lincoln's face was asymmetrical. This anatomical reality becomes clear when one views Civil War photographer Alexander Gardner's head-on "Gettysburg Portrait" of Lincoln (see page 32), taken on November 8, 1863, just two weeks before he delivered the Gettysburg Address. Upon careful examination of the portrait, it becomes clear that his eyes are not focused on the same object, his left eye looks slightly upward. His right side is more solemn, with a sunken cheek, extended lower lip, and ominous glare. On his left side, however, he appears to have a slight grin, his lower lip tighter and more puckered.

Lincoln eventually recovered from his injury, but his family suffered a much greater tragedy later that year. In 1818 the Pigeon Creek community suffered an epidemic of "milk sickness" formally known as brucellosis, caused by drinking milk from cows that had eaten the poisonous snakeroot plant while grazing freely in the forest. Victims experienced dizziness, nausea, and stomach pains, followed by irregular respiration and heartbeat, extreme fatigue, and unconsciousness. Often victims did not survive. Thomas and Elizabeth Sparrow died in September, and Abraham's mother, Nancy Hanks Lincoln, died on October 5. With little fanfare, Thomas buried her in a coffin of rough pine boards on a wooded knoll near the cabin.

The next several months were difficult for the whole family. Dennis Hanks moved in with Thomas Lincoln and his two children to help provide for life's basic necessities, but their home became sad and cold. Albert Beveridge wrote, "Back to their doorless, windowless, floorless cabin, went Thomas Lincoln and his children; and there, with Dennis Hanks, they lived through the remainder of winter, through the spring, the summer and the autumn of 1819. Sarah, now in her thirteenth year, did the cooking." Thomas and Dennis Hanks hunted game for sustenance, and Abraham brought water from the spring or creek. Nancy's death led to a "year of squalor— mostly flesh for food, unfit water, wretched cooking, no knives or forks, bare feet, bodies partly clad, filthy beds of leaves and skins." Historians speculate about the lasting consequences of Lincoln's loss of his mother before he was ten years old. While his lifelong bouts with melancholy may not have stemmed directly from his childhood suffering, Lincoln himself remembered this period of his life with deep sadness. He would write in the 1840s upon visiting his Indiana home:

My childhood's home I see again,
    And sadden with the view;
And still, as mem'ries crowd my brain,
    There's pleasure in it too.

I hear the loved survivors tell
    How nought from death could save,
'Till every sound appears a knell,
    And every spot a grave.

I range the fields with pensive tread,
    And pace the hollow rooms,
And feel (companion of the dead)
    I'm living in the tombs.

Within a year of his wife's death, Thomas Lincoln journeyed back to Kentucky to find a new wife. He simply could not raise a family alone on the frontier. When he traveled back to Elizabethtown, he came into contact with Sarah (Bush) Johnston, a woman he had courted years earlier. She was now a widow, her first husband, Daniel Johnston, having died of the "cold plague" in 1814. She was left to raise her three children (John D., Sarah [Elizabeth], and Matilda) on her own. There was no romantic courtship or engagement. Sarah and Thomas simply needed one another. He agreed to pay her debts, and they married immediately. Sarah packed up her children and belongings, and they all traveled to Indiana where Abraham, Sarah, and Dennis Hanks waited in a windowless log cabin. Undernourished, melancholic from mourning the death of his mother, and unable to pursue an education, Abraham Lincoln was facing a future in peril.

Sarah Bush Johnston Lincoln (1788-1869), Lincoln's stepmother—a second pose. Ambrotype, probably taken in the 1850s or early 1860s, on display at the Stephenson County Historical Society in Freeport, Illinois. The pose differs from the most common Sarah Bush Lincoln photograph owned by Harriet (Hanks) Chapman. It is not clear who owned this photo, but the identification of the subject as "Sally Bush Abraham Lincoln's stepmother Thomas Lincoln's second wife" (found on the back of the picture) indicates that it was a close family member or friend. Historian Wayne C. Temple has argued that "There can be little doubt that it is a genuine picture of Lincoln's beloved stepmother." From the collection of the Stephenson County Historical Society, Freeport, Illinois.

Photograph taken by Alexander Gardner, November 8, 1863, just eleven days before Lincoln delivered the Gettysburg Address. Courtesy of the Abraham Lincoln Presidential Library & Museum.

CHAPTER THREE

Lincoln's Life on the Land: From Indiana to Illinois, and Beyond

The arrival in December 1819 of Sarah Bush Johnston Lincoln changed the Lincoln family's life profoundly. She brought with her all the trimmings of a proper home: bedding, a bureau, chairs, a spinning wheel, and eating utensils. Her children also brought new life into a sad household. But, most importantly, Sarah brought love, understanding, and motherly care. Dennis Hanks remembered her arrival, remarking, "She soaped—rubbed and washed the children clean so that they look[ed] pretty neat—well and clean." She took charge of the whole household. Under her direction, Thomas and Dennis Hanks split logs to make a cabin floor, completed the roof, fashioned a proper door, and even cut a hole for a window which they covered with greased paper to let in some light. Thomas, an experienced carpenter, constructed a new table and stools where the family dined together. Lincoln's new mother loved Abraham and his sister, Sarah, as her own children, growing especially fond of Abraham, whom she said was "the best boy I ever saw or expect to see." Starved for parental affection and care, Lincoln called her "Mama" and spoke of her for the rest of his life in nothing but affectionate terms. A relative remembered Lincoln describing Sarah as "his best friend in the world…and no man could have loved a mother more than he loved her." Her arrival changed everything for young Abe.

In the spring of 1820, Thomas and Sarah enrolled Abraham, his sister, and his three stepsiblings in Andrew Crawford's "blab" or "loud" school where they attended regularly for about three months. There, Abraham continued to learn reading, writing and "ciphering to single rule of 3 no further." Unfortunately, Crawford departed abruptly from the teaching profession. Lincoln attended school only sporadically for the next few years, with the longest stretch being six months in Azel W. Dorsey's school, which was housed in the same cabin Crawford had used.

By the time Lincoln was fifteen his formal education was over. He remarked in his 1860s campaign autobiography: "Abraham now thinks that the aggregate of all his schooling did not amount to one year." Lincoln always regretted his "want of education," but his insatiable desire to learn led him to read voraciously on his own. Years later, after he had left home and was living in New Salem, he continued his self-education, studying English grammar, reading the Greek classics, and learning law. Of himself Lincoln wrote, "He was never in a college or academy as a student, and never inside of a college or academy building till since he had a law license. What he has in the way of education he has picked up."

Abraham's stepsister Matlida recollected that "Abe was not energetic except in one thing—he was active and persistent in learning—read everything he could—ciphered on boards, on the walls." Dennis Hanks often referred to Lincoln's laziness, claiming that Abe "only showed industry in the attainment of knowledge." Lincoln read everything he could get his hands on, often frustrating his father who would have preferred that he be out in the fields working with his hands. Dennis Hanks and others recollected that Thomas often beat Abraham, and that the two simply looked at life from different angles.

Lincoln the boy, reading by the fire. Illustration by Lloyd Ostendorf.

Sarah had brought many books into the Lincoln home with her: *Robinson Crusoe, Pilgrim's Progress, Sinbad the Sailor, Æsop's Fables,* and the family Bible. Lincoln devoured them all. He also borrowed books from neighbors, like Grimshaw's *History of the United States* and Mason Weems's *The Life of George Washington.* Weems's text played a significant role in Lincoln's adolescent development. Eleanor Gridley, in her book *The Story of Abraham Lincoln,* recounts the story:

> One day when doing some work for his schoolmaster, Mr. Crawford, who had given up teaching and was not a citizen of the settlement, Abraham Lincoln found upon a table a copy of Weem's [*sic*] Life of Washington. This was a famous book in those days and the boy was very anxious to read it. Mr.

Crawford loaned the book to the lad with the injunction that if anything happened to it he would have to pay for it. With this possibility staring him in the face the boy was unusually careful, always placing the book out of reach by putting it on the top of the highest shelf. There was, however, a big crack between the logs back of the rude book-case and accidentally the book fell against the opening. During the night a severe rainstorm came up and when Abe awoke in the morning he found the book completely watersoaked. Mr. Crawford was a cross and cranky old man, and when Abraham Lincoln told him of the accident he stormed and scolded and said that he must "pull fodder for his cattle for three days." Although the boy considered the penalty unjust, he said not a word but complied with the demand, and it was in this manner that Abraham Lincoln paid for the first book that he ever owned.

Throughout his life, Lincoln would vigorously educate himself, even reading all of Euclid's works in the 1840s and '50s while at the height of his legal career.

As Lincoln reached his late teens, he ventured further and further from the farm, devising industrious ways to make money. At age sixteen he, along with Dennis Hanks and Squire Hall, attempted to sell firewood to the steamers traversing the Ohio River. He also hired himself out to James Taylor who ran a ferry across the Ohio. During his spare time he constructed his own rowboat, and it was this project that would change his life forever, allowing him to earn his first dollar on his own. Lincoln would recollect later in life,

[Y]ou never heard, did you, how I earned my first dollar? ... I was about eighteen years of age. ... I was contemplating my new flatboat ... when two men came down to the shore in a carriage with trunks .... "Will you," said one of them, "take us and our trunks out to the steamer?" ... I was very glad to have the chance of earning something. I supposed that each of them would give me two or three bits....I sculled them out to the steamboat. Each of them took from his pocket a silver half-dollar, and threw it on the floor of my boat. I could scarcely believe my eyes as I picked up the money.... [Y]ou may think it was a very little thing ... but it was a most important incident in my life. I could scarcely believe ... that I, a poor boy, had earned a dollar in less than a day,—that by honest work I had earned a dollar. The world seemed wider and fairer before me. I was a more hopeful and confident being from that time.

During his teen years, Abraham Lincoln separated himself more and more from his family, often working for wages away from the farmstead. Yet Lincoln did not keep for himself the money he earned from this work. Because he was under the age of twenty-one, he legally owed the money to his father. That being said, such experiences brought him away from the farm and introduced him to a whole new world of culture and commerce. In January of 1828, his sister, Sarah, died in childbirth. Lincoln was seventeen at the time and blamed her death on her husband's family's refusal to summon a doctor in time. As a result, he increasingly felt he could not get away from Pigeon Creek fast enough.

The following spring Lincoln accompanied the son of local store owner James Gentry on a flatboat trip to New Orleans. Lincoln brought Gentry's shipment of meat, corn, and flour to market in New Orleans and was paid eight dollars per month. He later recalled that at one point on that journey he and Allen Gentry "were attacked by seven negroes with intent to kill and rob them. They were hurt some in the melee, but succeeded in driving the negroes from the boat, and then 'cut cable' 'weighed anchor' and left." While in New Orleans, Abraham would have encountered large numbers of slaves for the first time, although he never made any formal record of this visit. In a few years, however, Lincoln would visit New Orleans again, and upon seeing the inhumane treatment of slaves at auction would pledge himself to rid the country of the unjust institution.

Shortly after Abraham returned to Indiana, his father made plans to move the whole family to Illinois. John Hanks, Nancy Hanks Lincoln's cousin who had lived in Pigeon Creek with Thomas and his family for four years, had moved on to Macon County, Illinois, in 1828. He sent back glowing reports of plentiful and fertile farmland and entreated the Lincoln family to join him and his family on the banks of the Sangamon River, not far from Springfield. Dennis Hanks, another cousin of Nancy Hanks Lincoln, decided to join the group, as did the family of Squire Hall, Dennis Hanks's half-brother. Leaving behind the land of the deadly "milk sickness," the party of thirteen migrants headed for Illinois to look for a new life.

Illinois had become a state only ten years earlier, in 1818. Its arable land and free institutions attracted small farmers to the central and southern portions of the state from Indiana, Tennessee, Kentucky, and other upcountry southern states where good land and opportunity were increasingly scarce. The land that made up Illinois had been part of the French Empire until the conclusion of the Seven Years War (or "French and Indian War") in 1763 when it became part of the British Empire. The British officially ceded the land to the new United States in September 1783 as part of the Treaty of Paris that ended the American Revolution. In the 1780s, Massachusetts, Connecticut, New York, and Virginia ceded their land claims in the Midwest (now Wisconsin, Illinois, and portions of Minnesota and Michigan) to the federal government. The government combined these into the Northwest Territory, and in the Ordinances of 1785 and 1787 established uniform procedures for surveying the land, as well as delineating territory boundaries and steps for achieving statehood. Early settlers clashed with Native American Indian tribes who resided in Illinois: Potawatomi, Kickapoo, Winnebago, Miami, Sauk, and Fox. These clashes culminated in the 1832 Black Hawk War in which Abraham Lincoln served as a captain in the Illinois militia. Threats against white settlers largely ceased as a result of the Black Hawk War which, when over, cleared the land for further settlement.

In March of 1830, a month after his twenty-first birthday, Abraham Lincoln moved with his family 120 miles from Spencer County, Indiana, to the banks of the Sangamon River in Macon County, Illinois, near the village

This map of Illinois is taken from the Universal Atlas published by Thomas, Cowperthwait & Co., Philadelphia, 1851—the year of Thomas Lincoln's death and ten years after Abraham Lincoln purchased the forty acres from his parents. This map shows the state coming into its own, depicting a burgeoning network of roads, railroads, and canals. Coles County is in the central, eastern portion of the state, just right of the second "I" in "ILLINOIS." Picture taken and map owned by author.

of Decatur. The oxen teams pulling a large wagon were able to make better time than they would have weeks later when the spring thaw softened the prairie soil. But the trip was still harrowing as the Lincoln clan made its way across the rough terrain of the newly opened frontier. Late in his life Dennis Hanks described the challenging voyage across the rough prairie this way:

> It tuk us two weeks to get thar, raftin' over the Wabash [River], cuttin' our way through the woods, fordin' rivers, pryin' wagons and steers out o' sloughs with fence rails, an' makin' camp. Abe cracked a joke every time he cracked a whip, an' he found a way out o' every tight place while the rest of us was standin' round scratchin' our fool heads. I reckon Abe an' Aunt Sairy [Sarah] run that movin', an' good thing the did, or it'd a ben run into a swamp and sucked under.

At one of the river crossings, Abraham's dog jumped from the wagon and fell through the ice. Lincoln recalled many years later, "I could not bear to lose my dog, and I jumped out of the waggon and waded waist deep in the ice and water[,] got hold of him and helped out and saved him."

After weeks of travel, having passed through Coles County along the way, the Lincoln and Hanks party arrived on the banks of the Sangamon River. Lincoln wrote in his campaign biography, "Here they built a log cabin, into which they removed, and made sufficient of rails to fence ten acres of ground, fenced and broke the ground, and raised a crop of sown corn upon it the same year." As he had done so many times previously, Lincoln picked up an axe, helping his father hew logs for a home, split rails for a fence, and clear land for farming. Lincoln stayed to help his family get settled, but he had no intention of remaining a farm laborer for the rest of his life.

That first year in Macon County was plagued with suffering and difficulty. During the first fall, many members of the family suffered from malaria, and the following winter was unusually severe, locals remembering

Lincoln prepares boards for the family's Macon County, Illinois, cabin in 1830. Illustration by Lloyd Ostendorf.

it as "the winter of deep snow." The first few months were so ominous that Thomas Lincoln decided to return to Indiana. In late spring 1831, Thomas and his family loaded up their wagons, intending to leave Illinois and return to Spencer County. Along the way, they once again traversed Coles County. While there, a local resident named John Sawyer persuaded Thomas and his extended family to settle there instead. So Thomas and Sarah, along with Dennis Hanks, Squire Hall, and their wives and children remained in Coles County. There, living on five different properties over the course of thirty years, Thomas and Sarah Bush Lincoln would reside for the rest of their lives.

Instead of accompanying the family to Macon County, Abraham and his stepbrother, John D. Johnston, together with John Hanks (Nancy Lincoln's cousin), contracted with Denton Offutt of Sangamo Town, a small community a few miles upriver from Springfield, to deliver a flatboat of produce to market in New Orleans. This was Abraham's second flatboat trip to the south, having taken Gentry's shipment to market in New Orleans three years earlier. On May 1, 1831, the three young men sailed down the Sangamon River on a flatboat of their own construction, eventually reaching the Mississippi which they followed to its mouth in New Orleans.

The trip began with a near catastrophe. Lincoln, Johnston, and Hanks had loaded the flatboat with bacon, corn, and hogs, but after only a few miles the boat became stranded on a milldam at the foot of a river bluff below the small town of New Salem. People from the community gathered to see what would happen as the craft took on water and threatened to sink. After they unloaded the supplies to another vessel, Lincoln drilled a hole in the bow of the boat, which allowed water to drain, thus causing the stern to rise up out of the water. The whole boat eventually lifted over the dam; and Offutt, who was watching from shore, was amazed at Lincoln's ingenuity. He vowed to open a store in New Salem upon Lincoln's return from New Orleans and to hire Lincoln as manager.

When they got to New Orleans, they visited a slave market. At the auction, Lincoln saw a mulatto girl sold. Hanks would recollect later that at that point, "the iron entered his soul," saying that Lincoln swore that if he ever got a chance to hit slavery, he would "hit it hard." When Lincoln returned to Illinois in the summer of 1831, he settled in New Salem; from there he moved on to Springfield in 1837 where he began his career as a lawyer and politician.

Meanwhile, Lincoln's parents had settled in Coles County. They had found forty acres in the "Buck Grove" neighborhood near the northwest corner of today's Pleasant Grove Township. Thomas Lincoln never obtained

Lincoln builds a flatboat for a trip to New Orleans in 1831. Illustration by Lloyd Ostendorf.

title to this land, instead squatting on it for three years until he purchased his "Muddy Point" farm from his stepson, John D. Johnston, in 1834. Abraham probably visited his parents at their Buck Grove home in late June or early July of 1831 after returning from New Orleans. History marks this visit by Abraham's wrestling match with Daniel Needham at Wabash Point. The 1907 *Lincoln Story Book* recounts the story this way:

> In 1831, Abraham Lincoln, returning from a voyage to New
> Orleans, paid the usual filial visit to his father, living in Coles
> County. A famous wrestler, one Needham, hearing of the
> newcomer's prowess in wrestling, more general than pugilism
> on the border, called to try their strength. As the professional

43

was in practice, and as the other, from his amiable disposition and his forbidding appearance was not so, the latter declined the honor of a hug and the forced repose of lying on the back. Nevertheless, taunted into trial, he met the champion and defeated him in two goes. The beaten one was chagrined, and vented his vexation in this defiance:

"You have thrown me twice, Lincoln, but you cannot whip me!"

"I do not want to, and I don't want to get whipped myself," was the simple reply.

"Well, I 'stump' you to lick me!" went on Needham, thinking he was gaining ground. "Throwing a man is one thing and licking him another!"

"Look here, Needham," said the badgered man, at last, "if you are not satisfied that I can throw you every time, and want to be convinced through a thrashing, I will do that, too, for your sake!"

The man "backed out." But he was afterward one of Lincoln's warmest friends.

A few weeks later, Lincoln arrived in New Salem, a hamlet of only fifteen log cabins. Denton Offutt had not followed through on his promise to open a store for Lincoln to manage; as a result Lincoln had no work. During the remainder of the summer of 1831 he earned small sums of money by taking odd jobs in the community, including piloting a small raft from New Salem to Beardstown for a Dr. Nelson who was relocating his family, along with all their personal belongings. Offutt eventually opened the store where Lincoln would serve as clerk.

Only weeks after his wrestling match with Daniel Needham in Coles County, Lincoln once again found himself having to prove himself in a feat of strength. New Salem was becoming a regional commercial village that supplied goods for surrounding rural areas like Clary's Grove and Concord. Because it was a trading center, it attracted farmers and workers from all around who came to town to grind their corn at the mill, stock up on supplies, or have a few drinks at the local "grocery" (a nineteenth-century term for a store that sold alcoholic beverages). In this rough-and-tumble frontier where men had to prove themselves, Jack Armstrong, leader of the "Clary's Grove boys" heard Denton Offutt claim that Abraham Lincoln was not just New Salem's smartest resident, but also its strongest. Armstrong and his roughneck followers were relatively innocent, free-spirited, rural young men who spent most of their free time in New Salem playing practical jokes, cockfighting, and ganderpulling (a competition where riders on horseback attempted to rip the head off a live goose suspended from a tree). Offutt bet Bill Clary, a local who ran a saloon near Offut's store, ten dollars that Lincoln could throw Armstrong, who was the local wrestling champion.

First Berry-Lincoln Store, now U. S. Post Office,
New Salem State Park, Lincoln's New Salem, Illinois

The First Lincoln-Berry Store in New Salem, Illinois. Brothers James and Rowan Herndon built this store building probably in the fall of 1831 and ran a general store. In 1832, James Herndon sold his interest to William F. Berry, and Rowan sold his interest to Abraham Lincoln, taking Lincoln's note in payment. Herndon wrote, "I believe he was thoroughly honest, and that impression was so strong in me, I accepted his note in payment of the whole. He had no money, but I would have advanced him still more had he asked for it." Lincoln and Berry opened a second store soon thereafter. The two eventually failed as grocers, and it took Lincoln years to pay off the debts he incurred during his years as a storekeeper. The building also served as a post office during the time Abraham Lincoln served as postmaster in New Salem from May 7, 1833, to May 30, 1836. Picture used with permission.

Carl Sandburg recounts the day's events:

> Sports from miles around came to a level square next to Offutt's
> store to see the match; bets of money, knives, trinkets, tobacco,
> drinks were put up. Armstrong, short and powerful, aimed from
> the first to get in close to this man and use his thick muscular
> strength. Lincoln held him off with long arms, wore down his
> strength, got him out of breath, surprised and "rattled." They
> pawed and clutched in many holds and twists till Lincoln threw
> Armstrong and had both shoulders to the grass. Armstrong's
> gang started toward Lincoln with cries and threats. Lincoln
> stepped to the Offutt store wall, braced himself, and told the
> gang he would fight, race or wrestle any who wanted to try him.
> Then Jack Armstrong broke the gang, shook Lincoln's hand,
> told them Lincoln was "fair," and "the best feller that ever broke
> into this settlement."

Other onlookers claimed it was a draw, and that after a long round of
hard tussling and trying different holds, Lincoln said, "Jack, let's quit. I can't
throw you—you can't throw me." One sure action everybody remembered
was that Armstrong gave Lincoln a warm handshake and they were close
friends ever after. The Clary's Grove boys called on Lincoln sometimes to
judge their horse races and cockfights, umpire their matches, and settle
disputes.

Lincoln quickly became a respected citizen of New Salem, living
amongst its residents for several years as a carpenter, riverboatman, store
clerk, soldier, merchant, postmaster, blacksmith, surveyor, lawyer, and
politician. He learned business skills and developed friendships that would
prepare him for the life of a successful lawyer and public servant.

In 1834, just three years after arriving in New Salem, Lincoln was elected
to the first of four consecutive two-year terms as that district's representative
to the Illinois General Assembly. He immediately began to study law on his

own, and received his license to practice law in 1836. The following year he was admitted to the Illinois bar. That same year, as one of the "Long Nine," a group of Sangamon County legislators, Lincoln succeeded in advocating to move the state capitol from Vandalia to Springfield where he immediately took up residence for good. Upon his reelection to the Illinois General Assembly the following year in 1838, Lincoln was named Whig floor leader. When he argued his first case before the Illinois Supreme Court in 1840, his status as a lawyer and politician grew. He married Mary Todd in 1842, and they moved into their new home at the corner of Eighth and Jackson in 1844. Two years later Lincoln was elected to the United States Congress, in 1846, where he served one term.

It was during these years of mounting legal and political success that Lincoln purchased "Lincoln's Farmland." He had left the laboring life of the

The Old State Capitol, Springfield, Illinois. This building housed the Illinois legislature from 1839 to 1876. Lincoln visited the building often both as a lawyer and state representative. He delivered his famous 1858 "House Divided" speech in Representatives Hall, and used the governor's rooms as a headquarters during the 1860 presidential campaign. Lincoln's body also lay in state in the building, May 3-4, 1865. The building was designated a National Historic Landmark in 1961 and was listed on the National Register of Historic Places in 1966. Photo taken by author, 2007.

farm far behind, yet he remained an Illinoisan firmly planted in the soil of the Midwestern prairie who lived out the virtues of hard work, frugality, and courage, which he had learned on the family farm. Lincoln remained a man of the land his entire life.

On the afternoon of April 14, 1865, just hours before his assassination, Lincoln took a long carriage ride alone with his wife. He had been reelected to the presidency the previous November, and one month earlier had delivered his Second Inaugural Address, which included some of history's most inspiring words.

Lincoln purchased this home at the corner of Eighth and Jackson Streets in Springfield, Illinois, in 1844. In 1855-56 the Lincolns added a second floor with three bedrooms and a master suite. When they moved to Washington D.C. in 1861, the home became rental property until 1887 when Robert Lincoln deeded the home to the state of Illinois for one dollar, asking only that it remain open free to the public. In 1972 the home was transferred to the National Park Service, which maintains it to this day.

With malice toward none; with charity for all; with firmness in the right, as God gives us to see the right, let us strive on to finish the work we are in; to bind up the nation's wounds; to care for him who shall have borne the battle, and for his widow, and his orphan—to do all which may achieve and cherish a just and lasting peace, among ourselves, and with all nations.

Lee's surrender at Appomattox Courthouse had occurred five days earlier, and Lincoln was thinking about what might come next. Carl Sandburg writes about that April afternoon: "As the carriage rolled along he talked about the next four years in Washington, how he hoped afterward perhaps for a trip abroad, then a return to Springfield, perhaps law practices and a prairie farm on the banks of the Sangamon." During his final hours, Lincoln was homesick for the Illinois prairie, the land of his young adulthood. Although his tragic, untimely death prevented him from fulfilling his dream, Lincoln seemed to imagine the quiet serenity of a small "prairie farm" where he might live out his remaining years in peace, sifting through his fingers the life-giving soil which had sustained him his entire life.

Abraham Lincoln and son Tad. Taken by Mathew B. Brady on February 9, 1864. Courtesy of the Abraham Lincoln Presidential Library & Museum.

For the information in chapter 4, the author relies heavily on previous historical research conducted by two Lincoln scholars. For a more complete treatment of this subject, see Charles H. Coleman, *Abraham Lincoln and Coles County, Illinois* (New Brunswick: Scarecrow Press, 1955, 28-78) ; and Harry E. Pratt, *The Personal Finances of Abraham Lincoln* (Springfield: The Abraham Lincoln Association, 1943), 58-70.

A History of Lincoln's Coles County Land: "Lincoln's Farmland"

braham Lincoln was never an aggressive real estate investor. He did buy and sell several plots of land, but not as a speculator intent on quickly turning an unjust profit in an expanding prairie town. In fact, many of his associates pointed out that he seemed almost indifferent to the acquisition of wealth. Joseph Gillespie, the Edwardsville lawyer who was closely associated with Lincoln, said he was economical without being parsimonious; and that though he did not engage in speculation, he was a hard-working and skilled businessman. Lincoln brought integrity to his business dealings, not interested in amassing only wealth, but wishing to make an honest buck by making sure to treat all parties fairly.

Land was central to Lincoln's vision for American character and growth. A "free soil" advocate, he came to abhor slavery, partly because it restricted land ownership to a few wealthy planters. As he became more financially secure, Lincoln made it a high priority to own his own land, not just to amass property, but in order to root himself in the local community and to refine the virtue of the free and equitable exchange of land and labor. Yet those values did not prevent him from making several savvy investments on lots in Illinois.

Lincoln's first ventures in land ownership began in 1836 when he received title to several lots in Huron, Illinois, as payment for survey work. He also took a portion of his payment from the Illinois legislature session in March 1836, to purchase a forty-seven acre tract of land on the bank of the Sangamon River one mile east of the planned town of Huron. (He eventually sold all this land.) That same month, he also purchased two housing lots in Springfield, selling each within a few weeks for a profit. In 1838, he purchased two more lots in Springfield across the street from the property he would purchase in 1844 for his own home. He retained ownership of these lots until the 1850s. Lincoln bought and sold land wisely, neither losing money nor benefiting wildly from a speculative market.

Lincoln's next purchase was "Lincoln's Farmland," a forty-acre portion of his parents' 120-acre Goosenest Prairie farm in Coles County. As noted earlier, Lincoln purchased this land on October 25, 1841, to rescue his father from financial difficulty, and then immediately gave use of the land back to his parents until their deaths. The fact that this was an act of filial piety as opposed to real estate investment is hinted at in a letter Lincoln wrote to his dear friend Joshua F. Speed on March 17, 1842, five months after he purchased the plot: "As to your farm matter, I have no sympathy with you. I have no farm, nor ever expect to have, and consequently have not studied the subject enough to be much interested in it." While Lincoln may have had farming in his past, he certainly did not think it would be in his immediate future. It was also clear that Lincoln never intended to profit from the land; at the time of purchase he also signed a bond agreeing to convey the land to John D. Johnston at any time within a year after the death of his last surviving parent, upon payment of $200—the exact amount Lincoln had paid for the land.

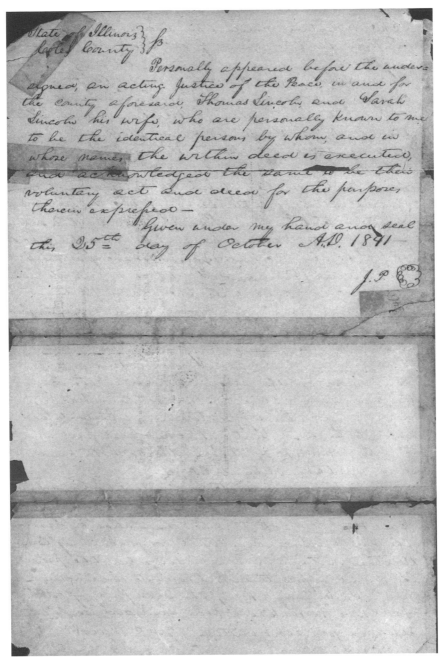

The original deed for "Lincoln's Farmland," recorded by Coles County recorder A. Ellington, October 25, 1841. Thomas Lincoln signed the deed, and Sarah Lincoln left her mark, an "X." Used with permission, Chicago Public Library, Special Collections and Preservation Division.

Deed, page 2.

This Indenture made this twenty fifth day of
October in the year of our Lord one thousand
eight hundred and forty one by and between
Thomas Lincoln and Sarah his wife, of the
county of Coles and State of Illinois, party of
the first part, and Abraham Lincoln of
the county of Sangamon and State aforesaid,
party of the second part Witnesseth: That the
said party of the first part, for, and in
consideration of the sum of two hundred
dollars to them in hand paid by the said
party of the second part, the receipt where=
of is hereby acknowledged, have granted, bar=
gained, and sold, and by these presents do grant,
bargain and sell unto the said party of
the second part, his heirs, and assigns, for=
ever, all the right, title, interest and estate
in and to the North East fourth of the South East quar-
ter of Section Twenty one in Township Eleven North, Range Nine East Containing forty
acres, more or less; reserving, however the occupa-
tion, use, and entire control, of said tract of
land and the appurtenances thereunto be=
longing to the said party of the first part, and
to the survivor of them, during both and
each of their natural lives—
To have and to hold to the said party
of the second part, his heirs and assigns for=
ever, subject to the reservation aforesaid
the above described tract or parcel of land,
together with all and singular the previ-
leges and appurtenances thereunto belonging—
In testimony whereof the said party of the first
part have hereunto set their hands and seals, the
day and year above written— Thomas Lincoln
                              Sarah her X Lincoln
                                     mark

Deed, page 3.

Thomas Lincoln had originally purchased what would become "Lincoln's Farmland" on December 31, 1840, from his stepson, John D. Johnston, who had purchased it from the federal government in August 1837. In so doing, Thomas grew his Coles County farm to 120 acres, but it turned out to be too much for him financially. In March of 1840, he had exchanged eighty acres north of "Lincoln's Farmland" for eighty acres to the west, which were owned by Reuben E. Moore, the husband of Sarah Bush Lincoln's daughter, Matilda. After this deal was completed, Thomas and John D. Johnston agreed to expand their living space by moving the cabin in which their families had been residing from "Lincoln's Farmland" to higher ground on the eighty acres newly acquired from Moore. They built a new cabin adjoining to the original, thus doubling their living space.

In his thorough 1955 book *Abraham Lincoln and Coles County, Illinois,* Charles H. Coleman asks, "Why did [Thomas] Lincoln make this exchange

Reuben Moore home. The Reuben Moore Home State Historic Site is located one mile north of the Lincoln Log Cabin State Historic Site in Lerna, Illinois. Reuben Moore bought the land on which the home stands in 1830. He built the home in 1856 and moved in with his wife, Matilda (Lincoln's stepsister), and five children from their previous marriages. It was in this home that Lincoln dined and said farewell to his mother in 1861 when he was on his way to take the oath of office as president. Picture taken by author, 2008.

of eighty acres with Reuben Moore?" In order to answer that question, Coleman engaged the investigative services of Byron K. Barton, head of the geography department at Eastern Illinois State College, who scrupulously examined the soil on both plots of land. In an extensive report, Barton reported that the original eighty acres Thomas had purchased was largely "upland prairie," difficult to farm in rainy years because of lack of drainage. The eighty acres owned by Moore which Thomas Lincoln desired was "well-drained forest soil and contained only three small acres of wet prairie." While modern farming techniques can more easily adjust to these land types, by mid-nineteenth century standards, Moore's land was significantly more desirable. Thomas Lincoln appeared to be exchanging his land for land that was more easily farmable. Thus Coleman's judgment was that the land deal reveals Thomas Lincoln's "good judgment as a farmer."

Coleman next considered whether or not Abraham Lincoln assisted his father and stepbrother in building the new double cabin they erected in the fall of 1840. There is no precise historical data answering this question. It is probable that Abraham was in Coles County that fall campaigning on the Whig ticket for his third term in the Illinois General Assembly. While it is impossible to pin this down with surety, tradition has Lincoln giving a speech in Charleston on September 30, so it is plausible that he assisted in erecting the cabin. If he was in Coles County in late September or early October, and if Thomas and Johnston were erecting the new cabin at that time, it is possible that Lincoln rode the seven or eight miles out to the Goosenest Prairie to assist them.

In fact, the exact year of the cabin's construction cannot be determined. One tradition claims that Thomas Lincoln lived in a rounded-log cabin on "Lincoln's Farmland" throughout the 1840s, and that the new double cabin on the land Thomas acquired from Reuben Moore was all new construction, not built until 1851 on the eve of Thomas Lincoln's death. Another local tradition holds that Thomas continued to live in the Johnston cabin on "Lincoln's Farmland" until 1849 when it was moved and expanded. Local resident William T. Phipps commented in 1950 that he had a conversation with John J. Hall, who claimed that Thomas and Johnston built the newer, larger cabin at Lincoln's urging. While theories abound, it is probable that Thomas Lincoln and John D. Johnston built their Goosenest Prairie cabin in 1840 with the help of family and friends, but probably not the help of Abraham Lincoln.

Regardless of whether Abraham Lincoln assisted in building the Goosenest Prairie cabin, he did come to his parents' financial rescue in October of 1841 when he purchased "Lincoln's Farmland." Such assistance would become a regular activity for Lincoln as he often provided for his parents. For example, in May 1845 he left a thirty-five-dollar fee he had collected from a client with the Coles County court clerk for his father to collect. While was serving as Illinois Representative in Washington D.C., he sent his father twenty dollars to keep his land from being sold. In that same letter, he responded to his stepbrother's request for eighty dollars, saying that Johnston's problem was "idleness," even offering to pay Johnston a dollar for every dollar he earned for five months. Lincoln grew weary of his father's and stepbrother's financial emergencies, at times communicating his frustrations in writing.

This fact raises the question, why did Abraham have to keep coming to his father's financial rescue? Historians over the years have provided several different possible answers. In her 1902 study, *The Story of Abraham Lincoln: On the Journey from the Log Cabin to the White House,* Eleanor Gridley described Thomas Lincoln as "lazy," "shiftless," neither "industrious nor enterprising," "good for nothing." Historian William E. Barton, in two important books on Lincoln's family published in the 1920s, came to mixed conclusions. He described Thomas as naturally indolent, lacking in ambition, and unwilling to regularly engage in hard labor. Further, he called Thomas "improvident and quite lacking in qualities that appeal to the imagination." Yet Barton also saw Thomas as having "good sense, sound judgment, a kind heart, and moderate ability"; even that he was "reliable and worthy of respect."

While many malign Thomas Lincoln's character, it is clear in the historical record that he paid his taxes regularly, left no unpaid debts, was remembered as a good neighbor, and that he worked a variety of jobs that demanded significant skill: farmer, carpenter, cabinetmaker, joiner, and mill operator. Perhaps historians have been so hard on Thomas Lincoln because as the myth of Abraham Lincoln grew, scholars sought to overemphasize his miraculous climb out rural poverty to political power, thus creating not only a humble beginning, but a morally bereft one. Such a starting place surely renders the rags to riches tale more dramatic.

Scholars also ascribe significance to the fact that Abraham Lincoln did not visit his father in December of 1850 when his father's health was declining, and that Lincoln did not attend his father's funeral in January of 1851. Biographer David Herbert Donald argues that Lincoln's refusal to go to his father's bedside at a minimum indicates that he could not "simulate a grief that he did not feel or an affection that he did not bear," and that "Thomas Lincoln represented a world that his son had long ago left behind him."

While it is true that Lincoln was sometimes critical of his father, it is also clear that he cared for and respected him. The previous summer when Thomas's health was failing Lincoln dropped what he was doing and rushed to his father's bedside.

In that case, Thomas quickly recovered, so when John D. Johnston again wrote Lincoln the following winter that his father was on death's door, perhaps Lincoln thought his stepbrother was once again overreacting. In addition, in the late fall of 1850 Mary Todd was pregnant with their son Tad and was bedridden with "baby-sickness." Lincoln was also still reeling from the death of their second son, Edward, who had passed away on February 1, 1850, from pulmonary tuberculosis. When Lincoln finally realized that his father was indeed seriously ill, he wrote to John D. Johnston explaining that the round trip, which would take one full week, was impossible. The full text of the letter is as follows:

Dear Brother,

On the day before yesterday I received a letter from Harriett, written at Greenup. She says she has just returned from your house; and that Father is very low, and will hardly recover. She also says you have written me two letters; and that although you do not expect me to come now, you wonder that I do not write. I received both your letters, and although I have not answered them, it is not because I have forgotten them, or been uninterested about them—but because it appeared to me I could write nothing which could do any good. You already know that I desire that neither Father nor Mother shall be in want on any comfort either in health or sickness while they live; and I feel sure you have not failed to use my name, if necessary, to procure a doctor, or any thing else for Father in his present sickness. My business is such that I could hardly leave home now, if it were not, as it is, that my own wife is sick-abed. (It is a case of baby-sickness, and I suppose is not dangerous.) I sincerely hope Father may yet recover his health; but at all events tell him to call upon, and confide in, our great, and good, and merciful Maker; who will not turn away from him in any extremity. He notes the fall of a sparrow, and numbers the hairs on our heads; and He will not forget the dying man, who puts his trust in Him. Say to him that if we could meet now, it is doubtful whether it would not be more painful than pleasant; but that if it be his lot to go now, he will soon have a joyous meeting with many loved ones gone before; and where the rest of us, through the help of God, hope ere-long to join them.

Write me again when you receive this. Affectionately.

A. Lincoln

In his request to Johnston to assure his father with the hope of heaven, Lincoln was addressing his father for the last time. Perhaps Lincoln did not understand the gravity of his father's illness, or perhaps his own grief and demanding schedule made an impromptu visit impossible. Some historians have argued that Lincoln's letter had an "unconvincing tone" and that Lincoln had no real affection for his father. Yet his lifelong commitment to family belies such a claim. In the end, Abraham Lincoln did not attend his father's funeral because of his wife's sickness, his own ongoing melancholy over his son's recent death, and a demanding schedule which did not allow for an impromptu week away from Springfield. While Lincoln's relationship with his father was indeed strained at times, it is a historical reach to say it was broken and sour; and the fact that he did not come to his father's deathbed, having been to see him only months earlier, does not prove he was shamefully leaving his family behind.

Abraham was probably more frustrated with his stepbrother than he was with his father. Some of Thomas's financial failures can be ascribed to his own poor decisions, and some to the daily struggle of life in the prairie. But he was also held back by his association with his stepson, John D. Johnston. There is little debate over Johnston's character. Most historians agree that he was lazy and un-enterprising. While living in Coles County, Thomas Lincoln was a defendant in five legal cases, and lost all of them— Johnston was involved in each case. It was the poor judgment of both Johnston and Dennis Hanks that led to the failure of Thomas Lincoln's grist mill operation. If Thomas Lincoln was guilty of bad decision making, he was also guilty of fidelity to his shiftless family members for whom he was, as historian Charles Coleman put it, left "holding the sack." Coleman argues in the end that Thomas Lincoln was more of a substantial citizen than many give him credit for. He owned significant real estate, served on juries in Kentucky, and was an upstanding member of the Coles County community.

While Lincoln maintained a generally pleasant relationship with his stepbrother, their relationship suffered significantly after the death of Thomas Lincoln on January 17, 1851. After Lincoln purchased "Lincoln's Farmland," legal suits and financial crisis followed for Thomas—each having to do with John D. Johnston's failure to pay debts and Thomas's being held responsible as a co-defendant. At one point, Lincoln's father even had to mortgage the eastern half of his remaining eighty acres to satisfy a debt left unpaid by his stepson. One month after Thomas died, Abraham conveyed his interest in the west eighty acres to Johnston for a nominal consideration, subject of course to his stepmother's dower right. Shortly thereafter, Johnston made plans to sell the land and move to Missouri in search of new environs and quick riches. Lincoln, deeply rooted in Illinois and quite concerned for his stepmother's well-being, wrote his stepbrother and quite heavy-handedly communicated his frustrations with Johnston's apparent shiftlessness.

> When I came to Charleston day before yesterday, I learned that you are anxious to sell the land where you live and move to Missouri. I have been thinking of this ever since, and cannot but think such a notion is utterly foolish. What can you do in Missouri better than here? Is the land any richer? Can you there, any more than here, raise corn and wheat and oats without work? Will anybody there, more than here, do your work for you? If you intend to go to work, there is no better place than right where you are; if you do not intend to go to work, you cannot get along anywhere. Squirming and crawling about from place to place can do no good. You have raised no corn this year; and what you really want is to sell the land, get the money, and spend it. Part with the land you have, and, my life upon it, you will never own a spot big enough to bury you in. Half you will get for the land you will spend in moving to Missouri, and the other half you will eat, drink, and wear out,

and no foot of land will be bought. Now, I feel it my duty to have no hand in such a piece of foolery. I feel that it is so even on your own account, and particularly on mother's account. The eastern forty acres I intend to keep for mother while she lives; if you will not cultivate it, it will rent for enough to support her— at least it will rent for something. Her dower in the other two forties she can let you have, and no thanks to me. Now, do not misunderstand this letter: I do not write it in any unkindness. I write it in order, if possible, to get you to face the truth, which truth is, you are destitute because you have idled away all your time. Your thousand pretences for not getting along better are all nonsense; they deceive nobody but yourself. Go to work, is the only cure for your case.

In this letter, Lincoln's understanding of land and labor is clear. It is an understanding that would come to dominate the Republican Party as it developed in the late 1850s, and one which propelled the United States into an industrial future at the conclusion of the Civil War. Lincoln affirmed a producer ethic which extolled the virtues of free, independent, and propertied working men. Even if one owned nothing but one's own labor, at least one could sell that for profit and make a future for self and family by eventually coming to own land. The United States, in this vision, was to be made up of free persons who owned their own labor and land. Clearly, such a vision made no room for slavery—or persons who refused to work. For Lincoln, as for other free soil advocates, land ownership, agricultural production, and industrial growth were at the center of the country's economic future. These, combined with the virtues of hard work, thrift, fair exchange, and moderation, would allow the United States to become the nation its founders intended. By encouraging Johnston to live well, Lincoln was revealing the politician and person he was becoming.

Johnston ignored Lincoln's advice. He convinced Sarah Bush Lincoln to relinquish her dower right. On August 12, 1851, Abraham Lincoln sold the eighty-acre Goosenest Prairie Farm he had just inherited from his father to his stepbrother for one dollar. On November 27, Johnston sold the property to John J. Hall, Sarah Lincoln's grandson, for $250. Even after receiving Lincoln's letter, Johnston continued to try to get Lincoln to allow him to sell the east forty, "Lincoln's Farmland." Lincoln communicated clearly to Johnston what he thought of his plan:

> Your proposal about selling the east forty acres of land is all that I want or could claim for myself; but I am not satisfied with it on mother's account. I want her to have her living, and I feel that it is my duty, to some extent, to see that she is not wronged. She had a right of dower (that is, the use of one-third for life) in the other two forties; but, it seems she has already let you take that, hook and line. She now has the use of the whole of the east forty, as long as she lives; and if it be sold, of course she is entitled to the interest on all the money it brings, as long as she lives; but you propose to sell it for three hundred dollars, take one hundred away with you, and leave her two hundred at 8 per cent, making her an enormous sum of 16 dollars per year. Now if you are satisfied with treating her in that way, I am not. It is true, that you are to have that forty for two hundred dollars, at mother's death; but you are not to have it before. I am confident that land can be made to produce for mother at least $30 a year, and I can not, to oblige any living person, consent that she shall be put on an allowance of sixteen dollars a year.

In February of 1852, Johnston migrated to Marion County, Arkansas, in the Ozarks. He stayed only one year before returning to Coles County where he died on April 1, 1854. His life became for Abraham Lincoln a testament to the dangers of idleness and financial speculation.

As indicated previously, Lincoln never sold "Lincoln's Farmland." In order to provide for his mother's financial well-being, he kept the land until his death; and legal title to the land did not pass to another person until 1888 when John J. Hall acquired it. Since purchasing the eighty acres in 1851, Hall had been cultivating "Lincoln's Farmland" alongside that land for more than thirty years. In 1891, Hall sold the 36/100 of an acre surrounding the family cabin to the Lincoln Log Cabin Association for $200 (he had already sold the cabin itself to James W. Craig of Mattoon for $1,000, who in turn sold it to the Association for $10,000). The cabin was dismantled and shipped to Chicago for the Columbian Exposition, or 1893 World's Fair. After standing for a year just outside the fairgrounds, it was dismantled and lost to history forever. In 1892, the Lincoln Log Cabin Association sold the Coles County cabin site to M. E. Dunlap for $1,000. Upon his death, the 36/100-acre cabin site became the property of Erskine S. Dunlap who, on January 1, 1929, conveyed it to Eleanor Gridley, former secretary of the Lincoln Log Cabin Association, for one dollar. She, in her own words, gave the land to the state of Illinois "without money or price," although there is no formal record of this land transaction.

The eighty acres of the original Goosenest Prairie farm and six acres from the western side of "Lincoln's Farmland" were acquired by the state of Illinois in 1929-1930. When John J. Hall died in 1909, the three "forties" went to his heirs: Squire Hall obtained thirty-four acres on the west side. On March 20, 1928, Squire Hall sold that parcel to Benjamin Weir, acting for the Charleston Chamber of Commerce, who in turn sold it to the state of Illinois on June 18, 1929. The remaining six acres of that forty-acre parcel, and twenty-eight acres west of it went to another son, Abraham Lincoln Hall; he sold those thirty-four acres to last resident William T. Phipps. Following its transfer to Emma W. Phipps, the property was sold to the state on June 28, 1929. Harriet Hall Martin obtained the remaining twelve acres of the second forty, as well as six acres on the western side of "Lincoln's Farmland." Following her death, her husband, John D. Martin, sold the twelve remaining acres of the second forty, and six acres on the west side of "Lincoln's Farmland" to the state of Illinois on December 17, 1930. This land contained the cabin site which Eleanor Gridley obtained from Erskine S. Dunlap in 1929; and although there is no formal deed indicating that she did give the land to the state, that 36/100-acre plot went to the state of Illinois as well.

Following the acquisition of the eighty-six-acre tract, the property became the "Lincoln Log Cabin State Park" (now known as the "Lincoln Log Cabin State Historic Site"). The federal government, in cooperation with the state of Illinois, established a Civilian Conservation Corps camp on the site. Workers designed and erected a replica of the original cabin, which stands to this day. They also constructed an "ash hopper" of the type pioneers used to make soap, along with a root cellar and a round-log barn, which has since been removed. They added rail fences to make the park appear historically authentic, and the park was dedicated on August 27, 1936. The Lincoln Log Cabin State Historic Site is now a vital component of Coles County tourism. It maintains not only the replica cabin built in the 1930s, but a visitors' center which houses a permanent museum. The site also includes the Sargent farm—a local farm that was moved and restored and now functions as a living farm where visitors can see how people lived and worked in the 1840s. The site also sponsors online and live educational programs for people of all ages.

"Lincoln's Farmland" has its own history of ownership. In his article "Thomas and Abraham Lincoln as Farmers," Wayne C. Temple, chief deputy director of the Illinois State Archives, details the progression of land ownership from the 1860s through the 1970s. When he purchased the land in 1841, Lincoln drew up a bond regarding future dispossession of the land:

> Now I bind myself, my heirs and assigns, to convey said tract of
> land to John D. Johnson, or his heirs, at any time after the death

of the survivor of the said Thomas Lincoln & wife, provided he shall pay me, my heirs or assigns, the said sum of two hundred dollars, at any time within one year after the death of the survivor of the said Thomas Lincoln & wife, and the same may be paid without interest except after the death of the survivor as aforesaid.

Despite the fact that Sarah Bush Lincoln was still living, the heirs of John D. Johnston gave a quit claim deed to Thomas L. D. Johnston for "Lincoln's Farmland" on August 31, 1866, being paid the sum of $500. Although no one can be sure, it is possible that Lincoln's stepmother knew nothing of the sale. While they could have argued legal title to the land, none of Abraham Lincoln's surviving heirs made a move to seize the land. Thomas ("Tad") Lincoln died in 1871, and Lincoln's wife, Mary Todd Lincoln, died in 1882. Neither paid any attention at all to the land. Lincoln's only surviving son, Robert, made no effort to maintain ownership of the land, even in 1909

The Sargent Farm, on the grounds on the Lincoln Log Cabin State Historic Site. In the 1840s, Stephen Sargent owned a farm about ten miles from the Lincolns. The farm's buildings were moved to the Lincoln Log Cabin site, and now serve as a living farm, illustrating the progressive farming methods of the mid-nineteenth century. Picture taken by author, 2008.

after being made aware that he may have legally owned it.

Having purchased Thomas Lincoln's Goosenest Prairie farm from John D. Johnston in 1851, John J. Hall, made a formal legal move to possess "Lincoln's Farmland" on May 7, 1888. He had been cultivating the land alongside his eighty acres for thirty-seven years. In a sworn affidavit, Hall argued that he

> entered into possession of said tract of land on or about the year A.D. 1851 under the claim of ownership of the same, and has held actual, open, continued, uninterrupted, unquestioned, undisturbed, and peaceable possession thereof, adverse to all others from thence hitherto, and that he has regularly paid all taxes and assessments levied against the same during that period.

As a result of this claim, Hall became the undisputed owner of "Lincoln's Farmland." He died on April 4, 1909. His five living heirs divided up his estate, and "Lincoln's Farmland" was split between Joseph A. Hall, who received thirty-four acres, and his sister Harriet Martin, who received six acres along the west side of the parcel. As mentioned above, Martin's widower sold her six acres to the state of Illinois in 1930, and it became part of the Lincoln Log Cabin State Park. Joseph A. Hall and his wife, Gertrude E. Hall, conveyed their thirty-four acres to Lewis W. Ely by a warranty deed on September 24, 1914. Two months later, Ely deeded the property to Chauncey R. Bowman; and before the year was finished, the Bowmans sold the property to neighbor William T. Phipps on December 4, 1914. These thirty-four acres of "Lincoln's Farmland" have remained in private hands ever since. William T. Phipps died on February 9, 1967. When his estate was finally settled, one grandson, Raymond W. Phipps Jr., bought out the other heirs and secured title to the thirty-four remaining acres of "Lincoln's Farmland."

In January of 1989, Ron Best, a neighboring farmer, bought thirty of the remaining thirty-four acres at auction in Mattoon after the bank foreclosed on the land. Best said that the land would be used for "farming and farming only"—and indeed, the land is farmed to this day. To the east of the land now managed by Friends of the Abraham Lincoln Historical Farm LLC is a sea of thriving crops of corn and beans—a living testament to the productive land Lincoln owned and his family cultivated for generations.

What about the remaining four acres? After the foreclosure sale, Raymond Phipps and the stockholders in his Lincoln Land and Title Company maintained ownership of the four remaining acres of "Lincoln's Farmland." It was this parcel that Dan Arnold purchased in 2007. Taking into account the complicated history of "Lincoln's Farmland," Arnold sought to save the land and preserve it for future generations. His purpose was not to make money from the land, but to give it back to the public by selling penny-size sections of land with commemorative deeds, and using the proceeds from land sales for philanthropic purposes, supporting causes

John J. Hall and his family in front of the Lincoln "Goosenest Prairie" cabin, 1880s. Courtesy of the Abraham Lincoln Presidential Library & Museum.

Lincoln himself would have supported: education, literacy, statesmanship, leadership development, and entrepreneurship. After a sinewy 160-year history, "Lincoln's Farmland" will now be used in ways Lincoln and his ancestors would have supported. Friends of the Abraham Lincoln Historical Farm LLC now owns and operates the almost four-acre swath of land on the eastern boundary of the Lincoln Log Cabin State Historic Site, just off East County Road 030N in Lerna, Illinois. "Lincoln's Farmland" is legally described as the Northeast Quarter of the Southeast Quarter of Section Twenty-one (21) in Township Eleven (11) North, Range Nine (9) east of the Third Principal Meridian. Anyone can own a piece of this land and walk the land that Lincoln owned and held in special regard for the well-being of his family. *

* *To purchase a piece of the farm, visit www.lincolnfamilyfarm.com or call 1-888-OWN-FARM*

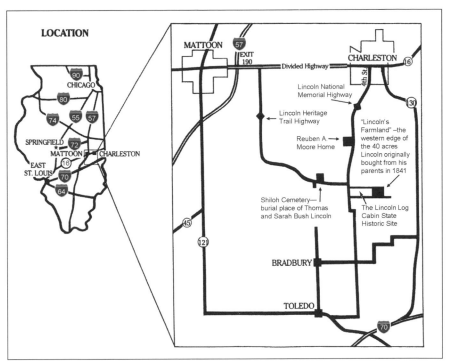

Map of Lincoln's land

Lincoln the grocer. This picture shows Abraham Lincoln behind the counter at the Berry-Lincoln store in New Salem, Illinois. Illustration by Lloyd Ostendorf.

The Lincoln Memorial, designed by Henry Bacon and opened for public viewing in 1922, stands 190 feet long and 119 feet wide, and is surrounded by thirty-eight Doric columns—one for each of the thirty-six states at the time of Lincoln's death, plus two at the entrance of the colonnade. The statue, carved by the Piccirilli brothers under the supervision of sculptor Daniel Chester French, is nineteen feet high and weighs 175 tons. Photograph used with permission.

Remembering Lincoln

On February 11, 1861, three weeks before he would take the oath of office in Washington D.C., Abraham Lincoln said good-bye to his friends and neighbors in Springfield, Illinois. As he boarded a special presidential train at the Great Western Railroad station, he looked out at a crowd of familiar faces and emotionally bid them farewell, saying,

> My friends, no one, not in my situation, can appreciate my feeling of sadness at this parting. To this place, and the kindness of these people, I owe everything. Here I have lived a quarter of a century, and have passed from a young to an old man. Here my children have been born, and one is buried. I now leave, not knowing when, or whether ever, I may return, with a task before me greater than that which rested upon Washington. Without the assistance of the Divine Being who ever attended him, I cannot succeed. With that assistance I cannot fail. Trusting in Him who can go with me, and remain with you, and be everywhere for good, let us confidently hope that all will yet

be well. To His care commending you, as I hope in your prayers you will commend me, I bid you an affectionate farewell.

Lincoln never returned. That same group of well-wishers would greet his coffin at the train depot four years later. His stepmother, Sarah, had predicted that her beloved Abe would never make it back home to Illinois. She was right. On April 14, 1865, Good Friday, Lincoln was shot and killed by John Wilkes Booth. He would never again walk the rolling hills of central Illinois where he had hoped to live out the rest of his life in pastoral simplicity.

When Lincoln was shot while watching a play at Ford's Theater in

Lincoln's Tomb at Oak Ridge Cemetery, Springfield, Illinois. The cemetery was dedicated in 1860. The 117-foot granite tomb was dedicated in 1874 Vermont sculptor Larkin Mead designed the tomb. Photograph by author, 2007.

Washington D.C., a group of soldiers who had been viewing the play carried his barely alive body to a private home across the street and laid him diagonally in a bed far too short for the six-foot-four president. While a young military doctor cared for him, anxious friends and family joined Mary Todd Lincoln as she wept in an adjoining room. When Lincoln died at 7:22 a.m. on Saturday, his deathbed was surrounded by members of his cabinet and other close friends and political allies. As Lincoln's elder son, Robert, wept, Rev.

Close-up of Larkin Mead's head of Lincoln at the Lincoln Tomb in Springfield, Illinois. Photograph by author, 2007.

Phineas D. Gurley, Lincoln's pastor, offered a brief prayer. Then Secretary of War Edwin M. Stanton spoke the now famous words, "Now he belongs to the ages."

After a military funeral, Lincoln's body was transported across the country along with the exhumed body of his son Willie; along the way, mourners held more than a dozen funerals. Lincoln's body eventually reached Springfield, Illinois, on May 3. It was interred at Oak Ridge Cemetery the following day. The Lincoln Tomb at Oak Ridge Cemetery was dedicated nine years later in 1874, and it holds the remains of Lincoln, Mary Todd Lincoln, and three of their four sons (Edward, William, and Thomas). Robert Lincoln is buried in Arlington National Cemetery in Virginia.

The reaction to Lincoln's death was swift and varied. While peace Democrats in the North ("Copperheads") and southerners rejoiced at his demise, communities throughout the North and Midwest draped their Main Streets in black. Although Easter dawned bright the morning after Lincoln died, history remembers that holiday as "Black Easter," with churches across the land covered in black tapestries and filled with worshipers wearing black mourning clothes. Pastors throughout the Union made sense of Lincoln's death in two ways. Some argued that because Lincoln had completed the work God gave him to do—namely freeing the slaves and winning the war—God took him to heaven so that sterner leaders more willing to punish the South for its wrongs could take over. Others argued that Lincoln's death was a national atonement for the sin of slavery and, as a result, the nation would be redeemed and have a brighter future. One poet referred to Lincoln's death as "freedom's eucharist." Many Americans believed Lincoln died for the sins of the American people so that the nation might again become great.

The martyred president immediately became mythic legend. Soon after his death, people began to couple Lincoln's name with George Washington's. Funeral banners declared, "Washington the Father, Lincoln the Savior." John Sartain's engraving "Abraham Lincoln the Martyr" included George Washington among the angels welcoming Lincoln into heaven. The famous lithographer Kimmel and Forster published a print entitled "Columbia's Noblest Sons," which showed Lady Liberty crowning Washington and Lincoln with laurel wreaths. Images of the Declaration of Independence, the Emancipation Proclamation, and several important historical events in the securing of freedom orbit the images of the deceased presidents (see page 79). Many even argued that Lincoln's body should be buried next to Washington's at Mount Vernon.

Americans appropriately revere Lincoln and honor him for the role he played in ending slavery, saving the Union, preserving the Constitution, and upholding the United States as the "last best hope for democracy." But they often go further, virtually deifying Lincoln as the perfection of all things properly American. As historian Merrill D. Peterson recounts in his book *Lincoln in the American Memory*, Americans have remembered Lincoln as the Savior of the Union, the Great Emancipator, a Man of the People, the First American, and a genuine Self-Made Man. In addition,

Kimmel and Forster, "Columbia's Noblest Sons," 1865. The images that surround Washington and Lincoln (beginning at the top left and moving counter-clockwise), include the Boston Tea Party, the signing of the Declaration of Independence, the surrender of Cornwallis at Yorktown, the Declaration of Independence, the Emancipation Proclamation, the Fall of Richmond, "Progress," and the siege of Fort Sumter. Library of Congress.

they have essentially attached to him words such as nationalism, humanity, democracy, Americanism, and individual opportunity. Lincoln is most certainly remembered by history as the greatest among presidents because he was prematurely martyred; as a result, it is at times difficult to find the real man among the many legends and myths.

When Americans gaze on Daniel Chester French's massive nineteen-foot sculpture of Abraham Lincoln at the Lincoln Memorial in Washington D.C., they would do well to remember that the savior of the Union began his life as a farm boy in Kentucky, and in many ways remained a man of the land his whole life. As Wayne C. Temple, chief deputy director of the Illinois State Archives, wrote, "Abraham Lincoln, quite naturally, never lost touch with farmers and farming. In his time, the bulk of his constituents lived in rural communities and on the farms of the Nation. These important hard-working citizens constituted the backbone of America. As a former Congressman [and Senator] Lincoln knew this fact extremely well." Consistent with this perspective, Lincoln declared in 1859 that seven-eighths of the labor done on northern farms was

> performed by men who labor for themselves, aided by their boys growing to manhood, neither being hired nor hiring, but literally laboring upon their own hood, asking no favor of capital, or hired labor, or of the slave. That is the true condition of the larger portion of all the labor done in this community [Cincinnati, Ohio], or that should be the condition of labor in well-regulated communities of agriculturalists.

Lincoln knew what he was talking about. He was one of those boys who grew to manhood on a farm. Like his father, he opposed slavery, believing that every American should be able to create a future through hard work on land that they owned. Although he left farming to become a store clerk, lawyer, and politician, Lincoln never really left the land behind. He came to his parents' financial rescue in 1841 by purchasing a forty-acre parcel of land so that he could return it to them as a free gift. He walked that land, "Lincoln's Farmland," in 1861 just before he left Illinois to take the presidential oath of office. He even dreamed of returning to his Illinois farmland when he left office. Throughout his life, Abraham Lincoln nurtured a connection to the land and the people who worked it. When one walks "Lincoln's Farmland" today, it is almost possible to hear Lincoln trudging through the prairie grass, axe in one hand and a book the other, dreaming of the day he might become great.

Illustration by Lloyd Ostendorf.

APPENDIX

LINCOLN FAMILY TREE

Daniel Johnston (d. 1816|)

Sarah (Bush) (Johnston) Lincoln (1788-1869)

Thomas Lincoln (1778-1851)

Nancy (Hanks) Lincoln (1784-1818)
Nancy's Aunt Elizabeth married Thomas Sparrow; they lived with the Lincolns in Indiana and, like Nancy, died of "milk sickness"

m. 1806

m. 1819

m. 1806

Sarah [Betsy] Elizabeth (Johnston) Hanks
• m. Dennis Hanks (cousin to Nancy Hanks Lincoln)
• Eight children

Matilda (Johnston) (Hall) Moore (1809-187̃8)
• m. Squire Hall
• Eight children, one of whom was John J. Hall
• Squire died, 1851
• m. Reuben Moore, 1856
• One Child, Giles

John D. Johnston (1810-1854)
• m. Mary Barker
• Seven children
• Mary died
• m. Nancy Williams
• One child: John D. Johnston, Jr.

Sarah (Lincoln) Grigsby (1807-1828)
m. Aaron Grigsby

Abraham Lincoln (1809-1865)
m. Mary Todd (1818-1882)

children:
• *Robert Todd (1843-1926)*
• *Edward (Eddie) (1846-1850)*
• *William (Willie) (1850-1862)*
• *Thomas (Tad) (1853-1871)*

Thomas Lincoln (1812-1814)

TIMELINE
of the Life of Abraham Lincoln

Dates relating to Lincoln's earlier life and "Lincoln's Farmland"

1778   Thomas Lincoln (Abraham's father) born in Rockingham, County, Virginia.

1784   Nancy Hanks (Abraham's mother) born in Hampshire County, Virginia.

1788   Sarah Bush (Abraham's stepmother) born in Elizabethtown, Kentucky.

1806   Thomas and Nancy Hanks Lincoln are married.

Daughter Sarah (Abraham's sister) is born to Thomas and Nancy Hanks Lincoln.

1809   On February 12, Abraham Lincoln is born in a one-room cabin in Hodgenville, Kentucky.

1810   Son Thomas born to Thomas and Nancy Hanks Lincoln.

1811   Lincoln family moves to a 230-acre farm on Knob Creek in Hodgenville, Kentucky.

1812   Thomas and Nancy Hanks Lincoln's son Thomas dies at two years of age.

1816   Lincoln family moves to Perry (later Spencer) County, Indiana.

1818   Abraham is kicked in the head by a horse and is thought to be dead.

Nancy Hanks Lincoln dies of "milk sickness."

1819   Thomas Lincoln marries Sarah Bush Johnston (her first husband, Daniel Johnston, had died in 1816).

1828   Sarah Lincoln (Abraham's sister) dies in childbirth.

Abraham and Allen Gentry take a flatboat of produce to market in New Orleans.

1830   Thomas Lincoln and his family, including Abraham, now twenty-one years old, travel two hundred miles to Illinois where they settle on the banks of the Sangamon River in Macon County.

1831　Abraham makes his second flatboat trip to New Orleans.

Thomas and Sarah Bush Johnston Lincoln move from Macon County to Coles County, Illinois.

Abraham moves to New Salem.

1832　Abraham serves in the Illinois militia during the Black Hawk War.

1834　Abraham elected to his first term in the Illinois General Assembly as a member of the Whig Party.

1836　Abraham reelected to the Illinois General Assembly and receives his license to practice law in the state of Illinois.

Abraham helps to get the state capitol moved from Vandalia to Springfield and settles in Springfield.

John D. Johnston purchases forty acres of farmland ("Lincoln's Farmland") in Coles County, Illinois, from the U.S. government.

Thomas and Sarah Bush Lincoln, and John D. Johnston, his wife, and their two boys move into a one-room cabin on the land.

1840　In June, Lincoln argues his first case before the Illinois Supreme Court and in August is reelected to the Illinois General Assembly.

Thomas Lincoln purchases the eighty acres adjacent to the western boundary of Johnston's land from Reuben Moore.

Thomas Lincoln and John D. Johnston move the cabin from Johnston's land to the new property, enlarging the cabin in the process.

On December 31, Thomas Lincoln purchases the land from John D. Johnston for $50.

1841　On October 25, Abraham Lincoln purchases the land from his father for $200, giving his parents exclusive use of the land until their deaths.

1846　Abraham elected as Whig candidate to serve as Illinois Representative in the United States House of Representatives.

1851　On January 17, Thomas Lincoln dies. Abraham inherits the west eighty acres, adjacent to the land he already owns.

On August 12, Abraham sells the west eighty acres to John D. Johnston for $1. Although Johnston seeks to purchase from Abraham the remaining land, Abraham refuses and the land remains in his name.

1865   On April 14, Lincoln is shot by John Wilkes Booth.

On April 15, Lincoln dies. Lincoln's stepmother, Sarah Bush, becomes sole heir to "Lincoln's Farmland."

1869   Sarah Bush Lincoln dies.

1888   Legal title to the land passes to John J. Hall, Sarah Lincoln's grandson.

1909   John J. Hall dies. His son, Joseph J. Hall, inherits the land.

1914   On September 24, Joseph J. Hall conveys the land to Lewis W. Ely by warranty deed.

In November, Lewis W. Ely deeds the land to Chauncey R. Bowman.

On December 4, Chauncey R. Bowman sells the land to William T. Phipps.

2007   On September 25, Friends of the Abraham Lincoln Historical Farm purchases the land from the Phipps family.

BIBLIOGRAPHY

This is not an exhaustive bibliography but a basic list of works that will introduce the specialist and non-specialist alike to the life of Abraham Lincoln, the history of Illinois, and Lincoln's family in Coles County, Illinois.

Basler, Roy P., ed. *Abraham Lincoln: His Speeches and Writings.* Cleveland: De Capo Press, 1946.

Beveridge, Albert J. *Abraham Lincoln, 1809-1858.* 2 vols. Boston: Houghton Mifflin, 1928.

Biles, Roger. *Illinois: A History of the Land and Its People.* DeKalb: Northern Illinois University Press, 2005.

Coleman, Charles H. *Abraham Lincoln and Coles County, Illinois.* New Brunswick, NJ: Scarecrow Press, 1955.

Coy, David Kent. *Recollections of Abraham Lincoln in Coles County, Illinois: Stories about His Family and Friends and a Guide to Historic Lincoln Sites.* Charleston, IL: Looking for Lincoln Committee, 2000.

Davis, James E. *Frontier Illinois.* Bloomington: University of Indiana Press, 1998.

Donald, David Herbert. *Lincoln.* New York: Simon & Schuster, 1996.

Easter-Shick, Nancy, and Bonnie Brooks Clark. *'Round the Town Square: Life in Downtown Charleston, Illinois 1830-1998.* Charleston, IL: Easter-Chick Publishing, 1999.

Gary, Ralph. *Following in Lincoln's Footsteps: A Complete Annotated Reference to Hundreds of Historical Sites Visited by Abraham Lincoln.* New York: Carroll & Graf Publishers, 2001.

Gridley, Eleanor. *The Story of Abraham Lincoln: Or the Journey from the Log Cabin to the White House.* Chicago: Lincoln Log Cabin Association, 1902.

Guelzo, Allen C. *Abraham Lincoln: Redeemer President.* Grand Rapids: William B. Eerdmans, 1999.

Hamilton, Charles, and Lloyd Ostendorf. *Lincoln in Photographs: An Album of Every Known Pose.* Norman: University of Oklahoma Press, 1963.

Herndon, William H., and Jesse William Weik. *Herndon's Lincoln: The True Story of a Great Life.* Springfield, IL: The Herndon's Lincoln Publishing Company, 1885.

The History of Coles County, Illinois. Chicago: William Le Baron, Jr. & Co., 1879.

Jensen, Richard J. *Illinois: A History.* Urbana: University of Illinois Press, 1978.

Kunhardt, Philip B., Jr., Philip B. Kunhardt III, and Peter W. Kunhardt. *Lincoln: An Illustrated Biography.* New York, Alfred A. Knopf, 1992.

Lind, Michael. *What Lincoln Believed: The Values and Convictions of America's Greatest President.* New York: Anchor Books, 2004.

Miller, William Lee. *Lincoln's Virtues: An Ethical Biography.* New York: Alfred A. Knopf, 2002.

Nicolay, John G., and John Hay. 10 vols. *Abraham Lincoln: A History.* New York: Century Company, 1890.

Oates, Stephen B. *With Malice Toward None: A Life of Abraham Lincoln.* New York: Harper and Row, 1977.

Ostendorf, Lloyd. *Abraham Lincoln: The Boy the Man.* Springfield, IL: Phillip H. Wagner, 1962.

Peterson, Merrill D. *Lincoln in American Memory.* New York: Oxford University Press, 1994.

Pratt, Harry E. *The Personal Finances of Abraham Lincoln*. Springfield, IL: The Abraham Lincoln Association, 1943.

Prokopowicz, Gerald J. *Did Lincoln Own Slaves? And Other Frequently Asked Questions about Abraham Lincoln*. New York: Pantheon Books, 2008.

Santella, Andrew. *Illinois History*. Portsmouth, NH: Heinemann, 2002.

Sandburg, Carl. *Abraham Lincoln: One Volume Edition,* including *The Prairie Years* and *The War Years*. New York: Harcourt, 1954.

Schwartz, Barry. *Abraham Lincoln and the Forge of National Memory*. Chicago: University of Chicago Press, 2000.

Steers, Edward, Jr. *Lincoln: A Pictorial History*. Gettysburg: Thomas Publications, 1993.

Temple, Wayne C. "Thomas and Abraham Lincoln as Farmers." Bulletin of the 55th Annual Meeting of the Lincoln Fellowship of Wisconsin, Historical Bulletin Number 53. Racine, WI: Lincoln Fellowship of Wisconsin, 1996.

Williams, Henry L., ed. *The Lincoln Story Book*. New York: G. W. Dillingham, 1907.

NOTES

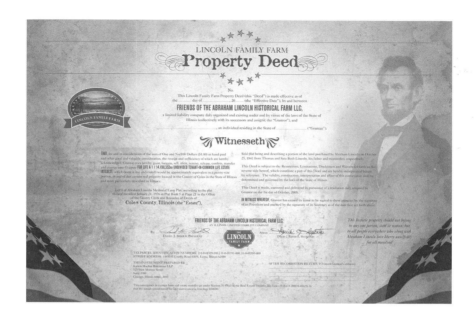

Friends of the Abraham Lincoln Historical Farm LLC has made it possible for you to own a portion of Lincoln's Land—a piece equivalent to the size of a penny, to represent the coin dedicated to our beloved former president. Along with your deed, you will receive a copy of this book, *Lincoln's Land: The History of Abraham Lincoln's Coles County Farm,* and a map with detailed directions to the farm. Your deed will be personalized with a unique serial number, date of purchase, name, and state of residence.

To purchase your own piece of Lincoln's Land, visit www.lincolnfamilyfarm.com, or call 1-888-OWN-FARM (or 1-888-696-3276).